A Bit O' Love

John Galsworthy

Contents

ACT I 7
ACT II 25
ACT III 43

A Bit O' Love

BY

John Galsworthy

ACT I

It is Ascension Day in a village of the West. In the low panelled hall-sittingroom of the BURLACOMBES' farmhouse on the village green, MICHAEL STRANGWAY, a clerical collar round his throat and a dark Norfolk jacket on his back, is playing the flute before a very large framed photograph of a woman, which is the only picture on the walls. His age is about thirty-five; his figure thin and very upright and his clean-shorn face thin, upright, narrow, with long and rather pointed ears; his dark hair is brushed in a coxcomb off his forehead. A faint smile hovers about his lips that Nature has made rather full and he has made thin, as though keeping a hard secret; but his bright grey eyes, dark round the rim, look out and upwards almost as if he were being crucified. There is something about the whole of him that makes him seen not quite present. A gentle creature, burnt within.

    A low, broad window above a window-seat forms the background to his figure; and through its lattice panes are seen the outer gate and yew-trees of a churchyard and the porch of a church, bathed in May sunlight. The front door at right angles to the window-seat, leads to the village green, and a door on the left into the house.

    It is the third movement of Veracini's violin sonata that STRANGWAY plays. His back is turned to the door into the house, and he does not hear when it is opened, and IVY BURLACOMBE, the farmer's daughter, a girl of fourteen, small and quiet as a mouse, comes in, a prayer-book in one hand, and in the other a glass of water, with wild orchis and a bit of deep pink hawthorn. She sits down on the window-seat, and having opened her book, sniffs at the flowers. Coming to the end of the movement STRANGWAY stops, and looking up at the face on the wall, heaves a long sigh.

    IVY. [From the seat] I picked these for yu, Mr. Strangway.

STRANGWAY. [Turning with a start] Ah! IVY. Thank you. [He puts his flute down on a chair against the far wall] Where are the others?

As he speaks, GLADYS FREMAN, a dark gipsyish girl, and CONNIE TRUSTAFORD, a fair, stolid, blue-eyed Saxon, both about sixteen, come in through the front door, behind which they have evidently been listening. They too have prayer-books in their hands. They sidle past IVY, and also sit down under the window.

Gladys. Mercy's comin', Mr. Strangway.

STRANGWAY. Good morning, Gladys; good morning, Connie.

He turns to a book-case on a table against the far wall, and taking out a book, finds his place in it. While he stands thus with his back to the girls, MERCY JARLAND comes in from the green. She also is about sixteen, with fair hair and china-blue eyes. She glides in quickly, hiding something behind her, and sits down on the seat next the door. And at once there is a whispering.

STRANGWAY. [Turning to them] Good morning, Mercy.

MERCY. Good morning, Mr. Strangway.

STRANGWAY. Now, yesterday I was telling you what our Lord's coming meant to the world. I want you to understand that before He came there wasn't really love, as we know it. I don't mean to say that there weren't many good people; but there wasn't love for the sake of loving. D'you think you understand what I mean?

MERCY fidgets. GLADYS'S eyes are following a fly.

IVY. Yes, Mr. Strangway.

STRANGWAY. It isn't enough to love people because they're good to you, or because in some way or other you're going to get something by it. We have to love because we love loving. That's the great thing—without that we're nothing but Pagans.

GLADYS. Please, what is Pagans?

STRANGWAY. That's what the first Christians called the people who lived in the villages and were not yet Christians, Gladys.

MERCY. We live in a village, but we're Christians.

STRANGWAY. [With a smile] Yes, Mercy; and what is a Christian?

MERCY kicks afoot sideways against her neighbour, frowns over her china-blue eyes, is silent; then, as his question passes on, makes a quick little face, wriggles, and looks behind her.

STRANGWAY. IVY?

IVY. 'Tis a man—whü—whü—

STRANGWAY. Yes?—Connie?

CONNIE [Who speaks rather thickly, as if she had a permanent slight cold] Please, Mr. Strangway, 'tis a man whü goes to church.

GLADYS. He 'as to be baptized—and confirmed; and—and—buried.

IVY. 'Tis a man whü—whü's glide and—

GLADYS. He don't drink, an' he don't beat his horses, an' he don't hit back.

MERCY. [Whispering] 'Tisn't your turn. [TO STRANGWAY] 'Tis a man like us.

IVY. I know what Mrs. Strangway said it was, cause I asked her once, before she went away.

STRANGWAY. [Startled] Yes?

IVY. She said it was a man whü forgave everything.

STRANGWAY. Ah!

The note of a cuckoo comes travelling. The girls are gazing at STRANGWAY, who seems to have gone off into a dream. They begin to fidget and whisper.

CONNIE. Please, Mr. Strangway, father says if yü hit a man and he don't hit yü back, he's no glide at all.

MERCY. When Tommy Morse wouldn't fight, us pinched him—he did squeal! [She giggles] Made me laugh!

STRANGWAY. Did I ever tell you about St. Francis of Assisi?

IVY. [Clasping her hands] No.

STRANGWAY. Well, he was the best Christian, I think, that ever lived—simply full of love and joy.

IVY. I expect he's dead.

STRANGWAY. About seven hundred years, IVY.

IVY. [Softy] Oh!

STRANGWAY. Everything to him was brother or sister—the sun and the moon, and all that was poor and weak and sad, and animals and birds, so that they even used to follow him about.

MERCY. I know! He had crumbs in his pocket.

STRANGWAY. No; he had love in his eyes.

IVY. 'Tis like about Orpheus, that yü told us.

STRANGWAY. Ah! But St. Francis was a Christian, and Orpheus was a Pagan.

IVY. Oh!

STRANGWAY. Orpheus drew everything after him with music; St. Francis by love.

IVY. Perhaps it was the same, really. STRANGWAY. [Looking at his flute] Perhaps it was, IVY.

GLADYS. Did 'e 'ave a flute like yü?

IVY. The flowers smell sweeter when they 'ear music; they dü.

[She holds up the glass of flowers. STRANGWAY. [Touching one of the orchis] What's the name of this one?

 The girls cluster save MERCY, who is taking a stealthy interest in what she has behind her.

CONNIE. We call it a cuckoo, Mr. Strangway.

GLADYS. 'Tis awful common down by the streams. We've got one medder where 'tis so thick almost as the goldie cups.

STRANGWAY. Odd! I've never noticed it.

IVY. Please, Mr. Strangway, yü don't notice when yü 're walkin'; yü go along like this.

[She holds up her face as one looking at the sky.

STRANGWAY. Bad as that, Ivy?

IVY. Mrs. Strangway often used to pick it last spring.

STRANGWAY. Did she? Did she?

[He has gone off again into a kind of dream.

MERCY. I like being confirmed.

STRANGWAY. Ah! Yes. Now—What's that behind you, Mercy?

MERCY. [Engagingly producing a cage a little bigger than a mouse-trap, containing a skylark] My skylark.

STRANGWAY. What!

MERCY. It can fly; but we're goin' to clip its wings. Bobbie caught it,
STRANGWAY. How long ago?
MERCY. [Conscious of impending disaster] Yesterday.
STRANGWAY. [White hot] Give me the cage!
MERCY. [Puckering] I want my skylark. [As he steps up to her and takes the cage—thoroughly alarmed] I gave Bobbie thrippence for it!
STRANGWAY. [Producing a sixpence] There!
MERCY. [Throwing it down—passionately] I want my skylark!
STRANGWAY. God made this poor bird for the sky and the grass. And you put it in that! Never cage any wild thing! Never!
MERCY. [Faint and sullen] I want my skylark.
STRANGWAY. [Taking the cage to the door] No! [He holds up the cage and opens it] Off you go, poor thing!

[The bird flies out and away. The girls watch with round eyes the fling up of his arm, and the freed bird flying away.

IVY. I'm glad!
MERCY kicks her viciously and sobs. STRANGWAY comes from the door, looks at MERCY sobbing, and suddenly clasps his head The girls watch him with a queer mixture of wonder, alarm, and disapproval.
GLADYS. [Whispering] Don't cry, Mercy. Bobbie'll soon catch yü another.
STRANGWAY has dropped his hands, and is looking again at MERCY. IVY sits with hands clasped, gazing at STRANGWAY. MERCY continues her artificial sobbing.
STRANGWAY. [Quietly] The class is over for to-day. He goes up to MERCY, and holds out his hand. She does not take it, and runs out knuckling her eyes. STRANGWAY turns on his heel and goes into the house.
CONNIE. 'Twasn't his bird.
IVY. Skylarks belong to the sky. Mr. Strangway said so.
GLADYS. Not when they'm caught, they don't.
IVY. They dü.
CONNIE. 'Twas her bird.

IVY. He gave her sixpence for it.

GLADYS. She didn't take it

CONNIE. There it is on the ground.

IVY. She might have.

GLADYS. He'll p'raps take my squirrel, tü.

IVY. The bird sang—I 'eard it! Right up in the sky. It wouldn't have sanged if it weren't glad.

GLADYS. Well, Mercy cried.

IVY. I don't care.

GLADYS. 'Tis a shame! And I know something. Mrs. Strangway's at Durford.

CONNIE. She's—never!

GLADYS. I saw her yesterday. An' if she's there she ought to be here. I told mother, an' she said: "Yü mind yer business." An' when she goes in to market tomorrow she'm goin' to see. An' if she's really there, mother says, 'tis a fine tü-dü an' a praaper scandal. So I know a lot more'n yü dü.

[Ivy stares at her.

CONNIE. Mrs. Strangway told mother she was goin' to France for the winter because her mother was ill.

GLADYS. 'Tisn't winter now—Ascension Day. I saw her comin' out o' Dr. Desart's house. I know 'twas her because she had on a blue dress an' a proud lüke. Mother says the doctor come over here tü often before Mrs. Strangway went away, just afore Christmas. They was old sweethearts before she married Mr. Strangway. [To Ivy] 'Twas yüre mother told mother that.

[Ivy gazes at them more and more wide-eyed.

CONNIE. Father says if Mrs. Bradmere an' the old Rector knew about the doctor, they wouldn't 'ave Mr. Strangway 'ere for curate any longer; because mother says it takes more'n a year for a glide wife to leave her 'usband, an' 'e so fond of her. But 'tisn't no business of ours, father says.

GLADYS. Mother says so tü. She's praaper set against gossip. She'll know all about it to-morrow after market.

IVY. [Stamping her foot] I don't want to 'ear nothin' at all; I don't, an' I won't.

[A rather shame-faced silence falls on the girls.

GLADYS. [In a quick whisper] 'Ere's Mrs. Burlacombe.

There enters from the house a stout motherly woman with a round grey eye and very red cheeks.

MRS. BURLACOMBE. IVY, take Mr. Strangway his ink, or we'll never 'ave no sermon to-night. He'm in his thinkin' box, but 'tis not a bit o' yüse 'im thinkin' without 'is ink. [She hands her daughter an inkpot and blotting-pad. IVY Takes them and goes out] What-ever's this? [She picks up the little bird-cage.

GLADYS. 'Tis Mercy Jarland's. Mr. Strangway let her skylark go.

MRS. BURLACOMBE. Aw! Did 'e now? Serve 'er right, bringin' an 'eathen bird to confirmation class.

CONNIE. I'll take it to her.

MRS. BURLACOMBE. No. Yü leave it there, an' let Mr. Strangway dü what'e likes with it. Bringin' a bird like that! Well I never!

The girls, perceiving that they have lighted on stony soil, look at each other and slide towards the door.

MRS. BURLACOMBE. Yes, yü just be off, an' think on what yü've been told in class, an' be'ave like Christians, that's güde maids. An' don't yü come no more in the 'avenin's dancin' them 'eathen dances in my barn, naighther, till after yü'm confirmed—'tisn't right. I've told Ivy I won't 'ave it.

CONNIE. Mr. Strangway don't mind—he likes us to; 'twas Mrs. Strangway began teachin' us. He's goin' to give a prize.

MRS. BURLACOMBE. Yü just dü what I tell yü an' never mind Mr. Strangway—he'm tü kind to everyone. D'yü think I don't know how gells oughter be'ave before confirmation? Yü be'ave like I did! Now, goo ahn! Shoo!

She hustles them out, rather as she might hustle her chickens, and begins tidying the room. There comes a wandering figure to the open window. It is that of a man of about thirty-five, of feeble gait, leaning the weight of all one side of him on a stick. His dark face, with black hair, one lock of which has gone white, was evidently once that of an ardent man. Now it is slack, weakly smiling, and the brown eyes are lost, and seem always to be asking something to which there is no answer.

MRS. BURLACOMBE. [With that forced cheerfulness always assumed in the face of too great misfortune] Well, Jim! better? [At the faint brightening of the smile] That's right! Yü'm getting' on bravely. Want Parson?

JIM. [Nodding and smiling, and speaking slowly] I want to tell 'un about my cat.

[His face loses its smile.

MRS. BURLACOMBE. Why! what's she been düin' then? Mr. Strangway's busy. Won't I dü?

JIM. [Shaking his head] No. I want to tell him.

MRS. BURLACOMBE. Whatever she been düin'? Havin' kittens?

JIM. No. She'm lost.

MRS. BURLACOMBE. Dearie me! Aw! she'm not lost. Cats be like maids; they must get out a bit.

JIM. She'm lost. Maybe he'll know where she'll be.

MRS. BURLACOMBE. Well, well. I'll go an' find 'im.

JIM. He's a güde man. He's very güde.

MRS. BURLACOMBE. That's certain zure.

STRANGWAY. [Entering from the house] Mrs. Burlacombe, I can't think where I've put my book on St. Francis—the large, squarish pale-blue one?

MRS. BURLACOMBE. Aw! there now! I knü there was somethin' on me mind. Miss Willis she came in yesterday afternüne when yü was out, to borrow it. Oh! yes—I said—I'm zure Mr. Strangway'll lend it 'ee. Now think o' that!

STRANGWAY. Of course, Mrs. Burlacombe; very glad she's got it.

MRS. BURLACOMBE. Aw ! but that's not all. When I tuk it up there come out a whole flutter o' little bits o' paper wi' little rhymes on 'em, same as I see yü writin'. Aw! my güdeness! I says to meself, Mr. Strangway widn' want no one seein' them.

STRANGWAY. Dear me! No; certainly not!

MRS. BURLACOMBE. An' so I putt 'em in your secretary.

STRANGWAY. My—ah! Yes. Thank you; yes.

MRS. BURLACOMBE. But I'll goo over an' get the büke for yü. 'T won't take me 'alf a minit.

She goes out on to the green. JIM BERE has come in.

STRANGWAY. [Gently] Well, Jim?

JIM. My cat's lost.

STRANGWAY. Lost?

JIM. Day before yesterday. She'm not come back. They've shot 'er, I think; or she'm caught in one o' they rabbit-traps.

STRANGWAY. Oh! no; my dear fellow, she'll come back. I'll speak to Sir Herbert's keepers.

JIM. Yes, zurr. I feel lonesome without 'er.

STRANGWAY. [With a faint smile—more to himself than to Jim] Lonesome! Yes! That's bad, Jim! That's bad!

JIM. I miss 'er when I sits thar in the avenin'.

STRANGWAY. The evenings—They're the worst—and when the blackbirds sing in the morning.

JIM. She used to lie on my bed, ye know, zurr. [STRANGWAY turns his face away, contracted with pain] She'm like a Christian.

STRANGWAY. The beasts are.

JIM. There's plenty folk ain't 'alf as Christian as 'er be.

STRANGWAY. Well, dear Jim, I'll do my very best. And any time you're lonely, come up, and I'll play the flute to you.

JIM. [Wriggling slightly] No, zurr. Thank 'ee, zurr.

STRANGWAY. What—don't you like music?

JIM. Ye-es, zurr. [A figure passes the window. Seeing it he says with his slow smile: "'Ere's Mrs.Bradmere, comin' from the Rectory." With queer malice] She don't like cats. But she'm a cat 'erself, I think.

STRANGWAY. [With his smile] Jim!

JIM. She'm always tellin' me I'm lükin' better. I'm not better, zurr.

STRANGWAY. That's her kindness.

JIM. I don't think it is. 'Tis laziness, an' 'avin' 'er own way. She'm very fond of 'er own way.

A knock on the door cuts off his speech. Following closely on the knock, as though no doors were licensed to be closed against her, a grey-haired lady enters; a capable, brown-faced woman of seventy, whose every tone and movement exhales authority. With a nod and a "good morning" to STRANGWAY she turns at once to JIM BERE.

MRS. BRADMERE. Ah! Jim; you're looking better.

[Jim Bere shakes his head.

MRS. BRADMERE. Oh! yes, you are. Getting on splendidly. And now, I just want to speak to Mr. Strangway.

JIM BERE touches his forelock, and slowly, leaning on his stick, goes out.

MRS. BRADMERE. [Waiting for the door to close] You know how that came on him? Caught the girl he was engaged to, one night, with another man, the rage broke something here. [She touches her forehead] Four years ago.

STRANGWAY. Poor fellow!

MRS. BRADMERE. [Looking at him sharply] Is your wife back?

STRANGWAY. [Starting] No.

MRS. BRADMERE. By the way, poor Mrs. Cremer—is she any better?

STRANGWAY. No; going fast. Wonderful—so patient.

MRS. BRADMERE. [With gruff sympathy] Um! Yes. They know how to die! [With another sharp look at him] D'you expect your wife soon?

STRANGWAY. I—I—hope so.

MRS. BRADMERE. So do I. The sooner the better.

STRANGWAY. [Shrinking] I trust the Rector's not suffering so much this morning?

MRS. BRADMERE. Thank you! His foot's very bad.

As she speaks Mrs. Burlacombe returns with a large pale-blue book in her hand.

MRS. BURLACOMBE. Good day, M'm! [Taking the book across to STRANGWAY] Miss Willis, she says she'm very sorry, zurr.

STRANGWAY. She was very welcome, Mrs. Burlacombe. [To MRS. BRADMERE] Forgive me—my sermon. [He goes into the house. The two women gaze after him. Then, at once, as it were, draw into themselves, as if preparing for an encounter, and yet seem to expand as if losing the need for restraint.

MRS. BRADMERE. [Abruptly] He misses his wife very much, I'm afraid.

MRS. BURLACOMBE. Ah! Don't he? Poor dear man; he keeps a terrible tight 'and over 'imself, but 'tis suthin' cruel the way he walks about at night. He'm just like a cow when its calf's weaned. T'as gone to me 'eart truly to see 'im these months past. T'other day when I went up to dü his rüme, I yeard a noise like this

[she sniffs]; an' ther' 'e was at the wardrobe, snuffin' at 'er things. I did never think a man cud care for a woman so much as that.

MRS. BRADMERE. H'm!

MRS. BURLACOMBE. 'Tis funny rest—an' 'e comin' 'ere for quiet after that tearin' great London parish! 'E'm terrible absent-minded tü—don't take no interest in 'is füde. Yesterday, goin' on for one o'clock, 'e says to me, "I expect 'tis nearly breakfast-time, Mrs. Burlacombe!" 'E'd 'ad it twice already!

MRS. BRADMERE. Twice! Nonsense!

MRS. BURLACOMBE. Zurely! I give 'im a nummit afore 'e gets up; an' 'e 'as 'is brekjus reg'lar at nine. Must feed un up. He'm on 'is feet all day, goin' to zee folk that widden want to zee an angel, they'm that busy; an' when 'e comes in 'e'll play 'is flüte there. He'm wastin 'away for want of 'is wife. That's what 'tis. An' 'im so sweet-spoken, til, 'tes a pleasure to year 'im—Never says a word!

MRS. BRADMERE. Yes, that's the kind of man who gets treated badly. I'm afraid she's not worthy of him, Mrs. Burlacombe.

MRS. BURLACOMBE. [Plaiting her apron] 'Tesn't for me to zay that. She'm a very pleasant lady.

MRS. BRADMERE. Too pleasant. What's this story about her being seen in Durford?

MRS. BURLACOMBE. Aw! I dü never year no gossip, m'm.

MRS. BRADMERE. [Drily] Of course not! But you see the Rector wishes to know.

MRS. BURLACOMBE. [Flustered] Well—folk will talk! But, as I says to Burlacombe—"'Tes paltry," I says; and they only married eighteen months, and Mr. Strangway so devoted-like. 'Tes nothing but love, with 'im.

MRS. BRADMERE. Come!

MRS. BURLACOMBE. There's puzzivantin' folk as'll set an' gossip the feathers off an angel. But I dü never listen.

MRS. BRADMERE. Now then, Mrs. Burlacombe?

MRS. BURLACOMBE. Well, they dü say as how Dr. Desart over to Durford and Mrs. Strangway was sweethearts afore she wer' married.

MRS. BRADMERE. I knew that. Who was it saw her coming out of Dr. Desart's house yesterday?

MRS. BURLACOMBE. In a manner of spakin' 'tes Mrs. Freman that says 'er Gladys seen her.

MRS. BRADMERE. That child's got an eye like a hawk.

MRS. BURLACOMBE. 'Tes wonderful how things dü spread. 'Tesn't as if us gossiped. Dü seem to grow-like in the naight.

MRS. BRADMERE. [To herself] I never liked her. That Riviera excuse, Mrs. Burlacombe—Very convenient things, sick mothers. Mr. Strangway doesn't know?

MRS. BURLACOMBE. The Lord forbid! 'Twid send un crazy, I think. For all he'm so moony an' gentlelike, I think he'm a terrible passionate man inside. He've a-got a saint in 'im, for zure; but 'tes only 'alf-baked, in a manner of spakin'.

MRS. BRADMERE. I shall go and see Mrs. Freman. There's been too much of this gossip all the winter.

MRS. BURLACOMBE. 'Tes unfortunate-like 'tes the Fremans. Freman he'm a gipsy sort of a feller; and he've never forgiven Mr. Strangway for spakin' to 'im about the way he trates 'is 'orses.

MRS. BRADMERE. Ah! I'm afraid Mr. Strangway's not too discreet when his feelings are touched.

MRS. BURLACOMBE. 'E've a-got an 'eart so big as the full müne. But 'tes no yüse expectin' tü much o' this world. 'Tes a funny place, after that.

MRS. BRADMERE. Yes, Mrs. Burlacombe; and I shall give some of these good people a rare rap over the knuckles for their want of charity. For all they look as if butter wouldn't melt in their mouths, they're an un-Christian lot. [Looking very directly at MRS. BURLACOMBE] It's lucky we've some hold over the village. I'm not going to have scandal. I shall speak to Sir Herbert, and he and the Rector will take steps.

MRS. BURLACOMBE. [With covert malice] Aw! I dü hope 'twon't upset the Rector, an' 'tis füte so poptious!

MRS. BRADMERE. [Grimly] His foot'll be sound enough to come down sharp. By the way, will you send me a duck up to the Rectory?

MRS. BURLACOMBE. [Glad to get away] Zurely, m'm; at once. I've some luv'ly fat birds.

[She goes into the house.

MRS. BRADMERE. Old puss-cat!

She turns to go, and in the doorway encounters a very little, red-cheeked girl in a peacock-blue cap, and pink frock, who curtsies stolidly.

MRS. BRADMERE. Well, Tibby Jarland, what do you want here? Always sucking something, aren't you?

Getting no reply from TIBBY JARLAND, she parses out. TIBBY comes in, looks round, takes a large sweet out of her mouth, contemplates it, and puts it back again. Then, in a perfunctory and very stolid fashion, she looks about the floor, as if she had been told to find something. While she is finding nothing and sucking her sweet, her sister MERCY comes in furtively, still frowning and vindictive.

MERCY. What! Haven't you found it, Tibby?
Get along with 'ee, then!

She accelerates the stolid TIBBY's departure with a smack, searches under the seat, finds and picks up the deserted sixpence. Then very quickly she goes to the door. But it is opened before she reaches it, and, finding herself caught, she slips behind the chintz window-curtain. A woman has entered, who is clearly the original of the large photograph. She is not strictly pretty, but there is charm in her pale, resolute face, with its mocking lips, flexible brows, and greenish eyes, whose lids, square above them, have short, dark lashes. She is dressed in blue, and her fair hair is coiled up under a cap and motor-veil. She comes in swiftly, and closes the door behind her; becomes irresolute; then, suddenly deciding, moves towards the door into the house. MERCY slips from behind her curtain to make off, but at that moment the door into the house is opened, and she has at once to slip back again into covert. It is IVY who has appeared.

IVY. [Amazed] Oh! Mrs. Strangway!

Evidently disconcerted by this appearance, BEATRICE STRANGWAY pulls herself together and confronts the child with a smile.

BEATRICE. Well, Ivy—you've grown! You didn't expect me, did you?

IVY. No, Mrs. Strangway; but I hoped yü'd be comin' soon.

BEATRICE. Ah! Yes. Is Mr. Strangway in?

IVY. [Hypnotized by those faintly smiling lips] Yes—oh, yes! He's writin' his sermon in the little room. He will be glad!

BEATRICE. [Going a little closer, and never taking her eyes off the child] Yes. Now, Ivy, will you do something for me?

IVY. [Fluttering] Oh, yes, Mrs. Strangway.

BEATRICE. Quite sure?

IVY. Oh, yes!

BEATRICE. Are you old enough to keep a secret?

IVY. [Nodding] I'm fourteen now.

BEATRICE. Well, then—I don't want anybody but Mr. Strangway to know I've been here; nobody, not even your mother. D'you understand?

IVY. [Troubled] No. Only, I can keep a secret.

BEATRICE. Mind, if anybody hears, it will hurt—Mr. Strangway.

IVY. Oh! I wouldn't—hurt—him. Must yü go away again? [Trembling towards her] I wish yü were goin' to stay. And perhaps some one has seen yü—They—

BEATRICE. [Hastily] No, no one. I came motoring; like this. [She moves her veil to show how it can conceal her face] And I came straight down the little lane, and through the barn, across the yard.

IVY. [Timidly] People dü see a lot.

BEATRICE. [Still with that hovering smile] I know, but—Now go and tell him quickly and quietly.

IVY. [Stopping at the door] Mother's pluckin' a duck. Only, please, Mrs. Strangway, if she comes in even after yü've gone, she'll know, because—because yü always have that particular nice scent.

BEATRICE. Thank you, my child. I'll see to that.

Ivy looks at her as if she would speak again, then turns suddenly, and goes out. BEATRICE's face darkens; she shivers. Taking out a little cigarette case, she lights a cigarette, and watches the puffs of smoke wreathe about her and die away. The frightened MERCY peers out, spying for a chance to escape. Then from the house STRANGWAY comes in. All his dreaminess is gone.

STRANGWAY. Thank God! [He stops at the look on her face] I don't understand, though. I thought you were still out there.

BEATRICE. [Letting her cigarette fall, and putting her foot on it] No.

STRANGWAY. You're staying? Oh! Beatrice; come! We'll get away from here at once—as far, as far—anywhere you like. Oh! my darling—only come! If you knew—

BEATRICE. It's no good, Michael; I've tried and tried.

STRANGWAY. Not! Then, why—? Beatrice.! You said, when you were right away—I've waited—

BEATRICE. I know. It's cruel—it's horrible. But I told you not to hope, Michael. I've done my best. All these months at Mentone, I've been wondering why I ever let you marry me—when that feeling wasn't dead!

STRANGWAY. You can't have come back just to leave me again?

BEATRICE. When you let me go out there with mother I thought—I did think I would be able; and I had begun—and then—spring came!

STRANGWAY. Spring came here too! Never so—aching! Beatrice, can't you?

BEATRICE. I've something to say.

STRANGWAY. No! No! No!

BEATRICE. You see—I've—fallen.

STRANGWAY. Ah! [In a voice sharpened by pain] Why, in the name of mercy, come here to tell me that? Was he out there, then?

[She shakes her head.

BEATRICE. I came straight back to him.

STRANGWAY. To Durford?

BEATRICE. To the Crossway Hotel, miles out—in my own name. They don't know me there. I told you not to hope, Michael. I've done my best; I swear it.

STRANGWAY. My God!

BEATRICE. It was your God that brought us to live near him!

STRANGWAY. Why have you come to me like this?

BEATRICE. To know what you're going to do. Are you going to divorce me? We're in your power. Don't divorce me—Doctor and patient—you must know—it ruins him. He'll lose everything. He'd be disqualified, and he hasn't a penny without his work.

STRANGWAY. Why should I spare him?

BEATRICE. Michael, I came to beg. It's hard.

STRANGWAY. No; don't beg! I can't stand it.

BEATRICE. [Recovering her pride] What are you going to do, then? Keep us apart by the threat of a divorce? Starve us and prison us? Cage me up here with you? I'm not brute enough to ruin him.

STRANGWAY. Heaven!

BEATRICE. I never really stopped loving him. I never loved you, Michael.

STRANGWAY. [Stunned] Is that true? [BEATRICE bends her head] Never loved me? Not—that night—on the river—not—?

BEATRICE. [Under her breath] No.

STRANGWAY. Were you lying to me, then? Kissing me, and—hating me?

BEATRICE. One doesn't hate men like you; but it wasn't love.

STRANGWAY. Why did you tell me it was?

BEATRICE. Yes. That was the worst thing I've ever done.

STRANGWAY. Do you think I would have married you? I would have burned first! I never dreamed you didn't. I swear it!

BEATRICE. [Very low] Forget it!

STRANGWAY. Did he try to get you away from me?

[BEATRICE gives him a swift look] Tell me the truth!

BEATRICE. No. It was—I—alone. But—he loves me.

STRANGWAY. One does not easily know love, it seems.

But her smile, faint, mysterious, pitying, is enough, and he turns away from her.

BEATRICE. It was cruel to come, I know. For me, too. But I couldn't write. I had to know.

STRANGWAY. Never loved me? Never loved me? That night at Tregaron? [At the look on her face] You might have told me before you went away! Why keep me all these—

BEATRICE. I meant to forget him again. I did mean to. I thought I could get back to what I was, when I married you; but, you see, what a girl can do, a woman that's been married—can't.

STRANGWAY. Then it was I—my kisses that—! [He laughs] How did you stand them? [His eyes dart at her face] Imagination helped you, perhaps!

BEATRICE. Michael, don't, don't! And—oh! don't make a public thing of it!

You needn't be afraid I shall have too good a time! [He stays quite still and silent, and that which is writhing in him makes his face so strange that BEATRICE stands aghast. At last she goes stumbling on in speech] If ever you want to marry some one else—then, of course—that's only fair, ruin or not. But till then—till then—He's leaving Durford, going to Brighton. No one need know. And you—this isn't the only parish in the world.

STRANGWAY. [Quietly] You ask me to help you live in secret with another man?

BEATRICE. I ask for mercy.

STRANGWAY. [As to himself] What am I to do?

BEATRICE. What you feel in the bottom of your heart.

STRANGWAY. You ask me to help you live in sin?

BEATRICE. To let me go out of your life. You've only to do—nothing. [He goes, slowly, close to her.

STRANGWAY. I want you. Come back to me!
Beatrice, come back!

BEATRICE. It would be torture, now.

STRANGWAY. [Writhing] Oh!

BEATRICE. Whatever's in your heart—do!

STRANGWAY. You'd come back to me sooner than ruin him ? Would you ?

BEATRICE. I can't bring him harm.

STRANGWAY. [Turning away] God!—if there be one—help me! [He stands leaning his forehead against the window. Suddenly his glance falls on the little bird-cage, still lying on the window-seat] Never cage any wild thing! [He gives a laugh that is half a sob; then, turning to the door, says in a low voice] Go! Go please, quickly! Do what you will. I won't hurt you—can't—But—go! [He opens the door.

BEATRICE. [Greatly moved] Thank you!

She passes him with her head down, and goes out quickly. STRANGWAY stands unconsciously tearing at the little bird-cage. And while he tears at it he utters a moaning sound. The terrified MERCY, peering from behind the curtain, and watching her chance, slips to the still open door; but in her haste and fright she knocks against it, and STRANGWAY sees her. Before he cari stop her she has fled out on to the green and away.

While he stands there, paralysed, the door from the house is opened, and MRS. BURLACOMBE approaches him in a queer, hushed way.

MRS. BURLACOMBE. [Her eyes mechanically fixed on the twisted bird-cage in his hands] 'Tis poor Sue Cremer, zurr, I didn't 'ardly think she'd last thrü the mornin'. An' zure enough she'm passed away! [Seeing that he has not taken in her words] Mr. Strangway—yü'm feelin' giddy?

STRANGWAY. No, no! What was it? You said—

MRS. BURLACOMBE. 'Tes Jack Cremer. His wife's gone. 'E'm in a terrible way. 'Tes only yü, 'e ses, can dü 'im any güde. He'm in the kitchen.

STRANGWAY. Cremer? Yes! Of course. Let him—

MRS. BURLACOMBE. [Still staring at the twisted cage] Yü ain't wantin' that—'tes all twizzled. [She takes it from him] Sure yü'm not feelin' yer 'ead?

STRANGWAY. [With a resolute effort] No!

MRS. BURLACOMBE. [Doubtfully] I'll send 'im in, then. [She goes. When she is gone, STRANGWAY passes his handkerchief across his forehead, and his lips move fast. He is standing motionless when CREMER, a big man in labourer's clothes, with a thick, broad face, and tragic, faithful eyes, comes in, and stands a little in from the closed door, quite dumb.

STRANGWAY. [After a moments silence—going up to him and laying a hand on his shoulder] Jack! Don't give way. If we give way—we're done.

CREMER. Yes, zurr. [A quiver passes over his face.

STRANGWAY. She didn't. Your wife was a brave woman. A dear woman.

CREMER. I never thought to lüse 'er. She never told me 'ow bad she was, afore she tuk to 'er bed. 'Tis a dreadful thing to lüse a wife, zurr.

STRANGWAY. [Tightening his lips, that tremble] Yes. But don't give way! Bear up, Jack!

CREMER. Seems funny 'er goin' blue-bell time, an' the sun shinin' so warm. I picked up an 'orse-shü yesterday. I can't never 'ave 'er back, zurr.

[His face quivers again.

STRANGWAY. Some day you'll join her. Think! Some lose their wives for ever.

CREMER. I don't believe as there's a future life, zurr. I think we goo to sleep like the beasts.

STRANGWAY. We're told otherwise. But come here! [Drawing him to the window] Look! Listen! To sleep in that! Even if we do, it won't be so bad, Jack, will it?

CREMER. She wer' a güde wife to me—no man cüdn't 'ave no better wife.

STRANGWAY. [Putting his hand out] Take hold—hard—harder! I want yours as much as you want mine. Pray for me, Jack, and I'll pray for you. And we won't give way, will we?

CREMER. [To whom the strangeness of these words has given some relief] No, zurr; thank 'ee, zurr. 'Tes no güde, I expect. Only, I'll miss 'er. Thank 'ee, zurr; kindly.

He lifts his hand to his head, turns, and uncertainly goes out to the kitchen. And STRANGWAY stays where he is, not knowing what to do. Then blindly he takes up his flute, and hatless, hurries out into the air.

ACT II

SCENE I

About seven o'clock in the taproom of the village inn. The bar, with the appurtenances thereof, stretches across one end, and opposite is the porch door on to the green. The wall between is nearly all window, with leaded panes, one wide-open casement whereof lets in the last of the sunlight. A narrow bench runs under this broad window. And this is all the furniture, save three spittoons.

GODLEIGH, the innkeeper, a smallish man with thick ruffled hair, a loquacious nose, and apple-red cheeks above a reddish-brown moustache, is reading the paper. To him enters TIBBY JARLAND with a shilling in her mouth.

GODLEIGH. Well, Tibby Jarland, what've yü come for, then? Glass o' beer?

TIBBY takes the shilling from her mouth and smiles stolidly.

GODLEIGH. [Twinkling] I shid zay glass o' 'arf an' 'arf's about yüre form. [TIBBY smiles more broadly] Yü'm a praaper masterpiece. Well! 'Ave sister Mercy borrowed yüre tongue? [TIBBY shakes her head]

Aw, she 'aven't. Well, maid ?

TIBBY. Father wants six clay pipes, please.

GODLEIGH. 'E dü, dü 'ee. Yü tell yüre father 'e can't 'ave more'n one, not this avenin'. And 'ere 'tis. Hand up yüre shillin'.

TIBBY reaches up her hand, parts with the shilling, and receives a long clay pipe and eleven pennies. In order to secure the coins in her pinafore she places the clay pipe in her mouth. While she is still thus engaged, MRS. BRADMERE enters the porch and comes in. TIBBY curtsies stolidly.

MRS. BRADMERE. Gracious, child! What are you doing here? And what have you got in your mouth? Who is it? Tibby Jarland? [TIBBY curtsies again] Take that thing out. And tell your father from me that if I ever see you at the inn again I shall tread on his toes hard. Godleigh, you know the law about children?

GODLEIGH. [Cocking his eye, and not at all abashed] Surely, m'm. But she will come. Go away, my dear.

TIBBY, never taking her eyes off MRS. BRADMERE, or the pipe from her mouth, has backed stolidly to the door, and vanished.

MRS. BRADMERE. [Eyeing GODLEIGH] Now, Godleigh, I've come to talk to you. Half the scandal that goes about the village begins here. [She holds up her finger to check expostulation] No, no—it's no good. You know the value of scandal to your business far too well.

GODLEIGH. Wi' all respect, m'm, I knows the vally of it to yourn, tü.

MRS. BRADMERE. What do you mean by that?

GODLEIGH. If there weren't no Rector's lady there widden' be no notice taken o' scandal; an' if there weren't no notice taken, twidden be scandal, to my thinkin'.

MRS. BRADMERE. [Winking out a grim little smile] Very well! You've given me your views. Now for mine. There's a piece of scandal going about that's got to be stopped, Godleigh. You turn the tap of it off here, or we'll turn your tap off. You know me. See?

GODLEIGH. I shouldn' never presume, m'm, to know a lady.

MRS. BRADMERE. The Rector's quite determined, so is Sir Herbert. Ordinary scandal's bad enough, but this touches the Church. While Mr. Strangway remains curate here, there must be no talk about him and his affairs.

GODLEIGH. [Cocking his eye] I was just thinkin' how to dü it, m'm. 'Twid be a brave notion to putt the men in chokey, and slit the women's tongues-like, same as they dü in outlandish places, as I'm told.

MRS. BRADMERE. Don't talk nonsense, Godleigh; and mind what I say, because I mean it.

GODLEIGH. Make yüre mind aisy, m'm—there'll be no scandal-monkeyin' here wi' my permission.

MRS. BRADMERE gives him a keen stare, but seeing him perfectly grave, nods her head with approval.

MRS. BRADMERE. Good! You know what's being said, of course?

GODLEIGH. [With respectful gravity] Yü'll pardon me, m'm, but ef an' in case yü was goin' to tell me, there's a rüle in this 'ouse: "No scandal 'ere!"

MRS. BRADMERE. [Twinkling grimly] You're too smart by half, my man.

GODLEIGH. Aw fegs, no, m'm—child in yüre 'ands.

MRS. BRADMERE. I wouldn't trust you a yard. Once more, Godleigh! This is a Christian village, and we mean it to remain so. You look out for yourself.

The door opens to admit the farmers TRUSTAFORD and BURLACOMBE. They doff their hats to MRS. BRADMERE, who, after one more sharp look at GODLEIGH, moves towards the door.

MRS. BRADMERE. Evening, Mr. Trustaford. [To BURLACOMBE] Burlacombe, tell your wife that duck she sent up was in hard training.

With one of her grim winks, and a nod, she goes.

TRUSTAFORD. [Replacing a hat which is black, hard, and not very new, on his long head, above a long face, clean-shaved but for little whiskers] What's the old grey mare want, then? [With a horse-laugh] 'Er's lükin' awful wise!

GODLEIGH. [Enigmatically] Ah!

TRUSTAFORD. [Sitting on the bench dose to the bar] Drop o' whisky, an' potash.

BURLACOMBE. [A taciturn, slim, yellowish man, in a worn soft hat] What's nüse, Godleigh? Drop o' cider.

GODLEIGH. Nüse? There's never no nüse in this 'ouse. Aw, no! Not wi' my permission. [In imitation] This is a Christian village.

TRUSTAFORD. Thought the old grey mare seemed mighty busy. [To BURLACOMBE] 'Tes rather quare about the curate's wife a-comin' motorin' this mornin'. Passed me wi' her face all smothered up in a veil, goggles an' all. Haw, haw!

BURLACOMBE. Aye!

TRUSTAFORD. Off again she was in 'alf an hour. 'Er didn't give poor old curate much of a chance, after six months.

GODLEIGH. Havin' an engagement elsewhere—No scandal, please, gentlemen.

BURLACOMBE. [Acidly] Never asked to see my missis. Passed me in the yard like a stone.

TRUSTAFORD. 'Tes a little bit rümoursome lately about 'er doctor.

GODLEIGH. Ah! he's the favourite. But 'tes a dead secret, Mr. Trustaford. Don't yü never repate it—there's not a cat don't know it already!

BURLACOMBE frowns, and TRUSTAFORD utters his laugh. The door is opened and FREMAN, a dark gipsyish man in the drees of a farmer, comes in.

GODLEIGH. Don't yü never tell Will Freman what 'e told me!

FREMAN. Avenin'!

TRUSTAFORD. Avenin' Will; what's yüre glass o' trouble?

FREMAN. Drop o' cider, clove, an' dash o' gin. There's blood in the sky tonight.

BURLACOMBE. Ah! We'll 'ave fine weather now, with the full o' the müne.

FREMAN. Dust o' wind an' a drop or tü virst, I reckon. 'Eard t' nüse about curate an' 'is wife?

GODLEIGH. No, indeed; an' don't yü tell us. We'm Christians 'ere in this village.

FREMAN. 'Tain't no very Christian nüse, neither. He's sent 'er off to th' doctor. "Go an' live with un," 'e says; "my blessin' on ye." If 'er'd a-been mine, I'd 'a tuk the whip to 'er. Tam Jarland's maid, she yeard it all. Christian, indeed! That's brave Christianity! "Goo an' live with un!" 'e told 'er.

BURLACOMBE. No, no; that's not sense—a man to say that. I'll not 'ear that against a man that bides in my 'ouse.

FREMAN. 'Tes sure, I tell'ee. The maid was hid-up, scared-like, behind the curtain. At it they went, and parson 'e says: "Go," 'e says, "I won't kape 'ee from 'im," 'e says, "an' I won't divorce 'ee, as yü don't wish it!" They was 'is words, same as Jarland's maid told my maid, an' my maid told my missis. If that's parson's talk, 'tes funny work goin' to church.

TRUSTAFORD. [Brooding] 'Tes wonderful quare, zurely.

FREMAN. Tarn Jarland's fair mad wi' curate for makin' free wi' his maid's skylark. Parson or no parson, 'e've no call to meddle wi' other people's property. He cam' pokin' 'is nose into my affairs. I told un I knew a sight more 'bout 'orses than 'e ever would!

TRUSTAFORD. He'm a bit crazy 'bout bastes an' birds.

  They have been so absorbed that they have not noticed the entrance of CLYST, a youth with tousled hair, and a bright, quick, Celtic eye, who stands listening, with a bit of paper in his hand.

CLYST. Ah! he'm that zurely, Mr. Trustaford.

[He chuckles.

GODLEIGH. Now, Tim Clyst, if an' in case yü've a-got some scandal on yer tongue, don't yü never unship it here. Yü go up to Rectory where 'twill be more relished-like.

CLYST. [Waving the paper] Will y' give me a drink for thic, Mr. Godleigh? 'Tes rale funny. Aw! 'tes somethin' swate. Bütiful readin'. Poetry. Rale spice. Yü've a luv'ly voice for readin', Mr. Godleigh.

GODLEIGH. [All ears and twinkle] Aw, what is it then?

CLYST. Ah! Yü want t'fknow tü much.

[Putting the paper in his pocket. While he is speaking, JIM BERE has entered quietly, with his feeble step and smile, and sits down.

CLYST. [Kindly] Hallo, Jim! Cat come 'ome?

JIM BERE. No.

  All nod, and speak to him kindly. And JIM BERE smiles at them, and his eyes ask of them the question, to which there is no answer. And after that he sits motionless and silent, and they talk as if he were not there.

GODLEIGH. What's all this, now—no scandal in my 'ouse!

CLYST. 'Tes awful peculiar—like a drame. Mr. Burlacombe 'e don't like to hear tell about drames. A guess a won't tell 'ee, arter that.

FREMAN. Out wi' it, Tim.

CLYST. 'Tes powerful thirsty to-day, Mr. Godleigh.

GODLEIGH. [Drawing him some cider] Yü're all wild cat's talk, Tim; yü've a-got no tale at all.

CLYST. [Moving for the cider] Aw, indade!

GODLEIGH. No tale, no cider!

CLYST. Did ye ever year tell of Orphus?

TRUSTAFORD. What? The old vet.: up to Dray-leigh?

CLYST. Fegs, no; Orphus that lived in th' old time, an' drawed the bastes after un wi' his music, same as curate was tellin' the maids.

FREMAN. I've 'eard as a gipsy over to Yellacott could dü that wi' 'is viddle.

CLYST. 'Twas no gipsy I see'd this arternune; 'twas Orphus, down to Mr. Burlacombe's long medder; settin' there all dark on a stone among the dimsy-white flowers an' the cowflops, wi' a bird upon 'is 'ead, playin' his whistle to the ponies.

FREMAN. [Excitedly] Yü did never zee a man wi' a bird on 'is 'ead.

CLYST. Didn' I?

FREMAN. What sort o' bird, then? Yü tell me that.

TRUSTAFORD. Praaper old barndoor cock. Haw, haw!

GODLEIGH. [Soothingly] 'Tes a vairy-tale; us mustn't be tü partic'lar.

BURLACOMBE. In my long medder? Where were yü, then, Tim Clyst?

CLYST. Passin' down the lane on my bike. Wonderful sorrowful-fine music 'e played. The ponies they did come round 'e—yü cud zee the tears runnin' down their chakes; 'twas powerful sad. 'E 'adn't no 'at on.

FREMAN. [Jeering] No; 'e 'ad a bird on 'is 'ead.

CLYST. [With a silencing grin] He went on playin' an' playin'. The ponies they never müved. An' all the dimsy-white flowers they waved and waved, an' the wind it went over 'em. Gav' me a funny feelin'.

GODLEIGH. Clyst, yü take the cherry bun!

CLYST. Where's that cider, Mr. GODLEIGH?

GODLEIGH. [Bending over the cider] Yü've a -'ad tü much already, Tim.

The door is opened, and TAM JARLAND appears. He walks rather unsteadily; a man with a heavy jowl, and sullen, strange, epileptic-looking eyes.

CLYST. [Pointing to JARLAND] 'Tis Tam Jarland there 'as the cargo aboard.

JARLAND. Avenin', all! [To GODLEIGH] Pint o' beer. [To JIM BERE] Avenin', Jim.

[JIM BERE looks at him and smiles.

GODLEIGH. [Serving him after a moment's hesitation] 'Ere y'are, Tam. [To CLYST, who has taken out his paper again] Where'd yü get thiccy paper?

CLYST. [Putting down his cider-mug empty] Yüre tongue dü watter, don't it, Mr. GODLEIGH? [Holding out his mug] No zider, no poetry. 'Tis amazin' sorrowful; Shakespeare over again. "The boy stüde on the burnin' deck."

FREMAN. Yü and yer yap!

CLYST. Ah! Yü wait a bit. When I come back down t'lane again, Orphus 'e was vanished away; there was naught in the field but the ponies, an' a praaper old magpie, a-top o' the hedge. I zee some-thin' white in the beak o' the fowl, so I giv' a "Whisht," an' 'e drops it smart, an' off 'e go. I gets over bank an' picks un up, and here't be.

[He holds out his mug.

BURLACOMBE. [Tartly] Here, give 'im 'is cider. Bade it yüreself, ye young teasewings.

CLYST, having secured his cider, drinks it off. Holding up the paper to the light, he makes as if to begin, then slides his eye round, tantalizing.

Clyst. 'Tes a pity I bain't dressed in a white gown, an' flowers in me 'air.

FREMAN. Read it, or we'll 'ave yü out o' this.

CLYST. Aw, don't 'ee shake my nerve, now!

He begins reading with mock heroism, in his soft, high, burring voice. Thus, in his rustic accent, go the lines:

God lighted the zun in 'eaven far, Lighted the virefly an' the ztar. My 'eart 'E lighted not!

God lighted the vields fur lambs to play, Lighted the bright strames, 'an the may. My'eart 'E lighted not!

God lighted the müne, the Arab's way, He lights to-morrer, an' to-day. My 'eart 'E 'ath vorgot!

When he has finished, there is silence. Then TRUSTAFORD, scratching his head, speaks:

TRUSTAFORD. 'Tes amazin' funny stuff.

FREMAN. [Looking over CLYST'S shoulder] Be danged! 'Tes the curate's 'andwritin'. 'Twas curate wi' the ponies, after that.

CLYST. Fancy, now! Aw, Will FREMAN, an't yü bright!

FREMAN. But 'e 'adn't no bird on 'is 'ead.

CLYST. Ya-as, 'e 'ad,

JARLAND. [In a dull, threatening voice] 'E 'ad my maid's bird, this arternüne. 'Ead or no, and parson or no, I'll gie 'im one for that.

FREMAN. Ah! And 'e meddled wi' my 'orses.

TRUSTAFORD. I'm thinkin' 'twas an old cuckoo bird 'e 'ad on 'is 'ead. Haw, haw!

GODLEIGH. "His 'eart she 'ath vorgot!"

FREMAN. 'E's a fine one to be tachin' our maids convirmation.

GODLEIGH. Would ye 'ave it the old Rector then ? Wi' 'is gouty shoe? Rackon the maids wid rather 'twas curate; eh, Mr. Burlacombe?

BURLACOMBE. [Abruptly] Curate's a güde man.

JARLAND. [With the comatose ferocity of drink] I'll be even wi' un.

FREMAN. [Excitedly] Tell 'ee one thing—'tes not a proper man o' God to 'ave about, wi' 'is lüse goin's on.

Out vrom 'ere he oughter go.

BURLACOMBE. You med go further an' fare worse.

FREMAN. What's 'e düin', then, lettin' 'is wife run off ?

TRUSTAFORD. [Scratching his head] If an' in case 'e can't kape 'er, 'tes a funny way o' düin' things not to divorce 'er, after that. If a parson's not to dü the Christian thing, whü is, then?

BURLACOMBE. 'Tes a bit immoral-like to pass over a thing like that. 'Tes funny if women's goin's on's to be encouraged.

FREMAN. Act of a coward, I zay.

BURLACOMBE. The curate ain't no coward.

FREMAN. He bides in yüre house; 'tes natural for yü to stand up for un; I'll wager Mrs. Burlacombe don't, though. My missis was fair shocked. "Will," she says, "if yü ever make vur to let me go like that, I widden never stay wi' yü," she says.

TRUSTAFORD. 'Tes settin' a bad example, for zure.

BURLACOMBE. 'Tes all very aisy talkin'; what shüde 'e dü, then?

FREMAN. [Excitedly] Go over to Durford and say to that doctor: "Yü come about my missis, an' zee what I'll dü to 'ee." An' take 'er 'ome an' zee she don't misbe'ave again.

CLYST. 'E can't take 'er ef 'er don' want t' come—I've 'eard lawyer, that lodged wi' us, say that.

FREMAN. All right then, 'e ought to 'ave the law of 'er and 'er doctor; an' zee 'er goin's on don't prosper; 'e'd get damages, tü. But this way 'tes a nice example he'm settin' folks. Parson indade! My missis an' the maids they won't goo near the church to-night, an' I wager no one else won't, neither.

JARLAND. [Lurching with his pewter up to GODLEIGH] The beggar! I'll be even wi' un.

GODLEIGH. [Looking at him in doubt] 'Tes the last, then, Tam.

Having received his beer, JARLAND stands, leaning against the bar, drinking.

BURLACOMBE. [Suddenly] I don' goo with what curate's düin'—'tes tü soft 'earted; he'm a müney kind o' man altogether, wi' 'is flute an' 'is poetry;

but he've a-lodged in my 'ouse this year an' more, and always 'ad an 'elpin' 'and for every one. I've got a likin' for him an' there's an end of it.

JARLAND. The coward!

TRUSTAFORD. I don' trouble nothin' about that,

TARN JARLAND. [Turning to BURLACOMBE] What gits me is 'e don't seem to 'ave no zense o' what's his own praperty.

JARLAND. Take other folk's property fast enough! [He saws the air with his empty pewter. The others have all turned to him, drawn by the fascination that a man in liquor has for his fellow-men. The bell for church has begun to ring, the sun is down, and it is getting dusk.] He wants one on his crop, an' one in 'is belly; 'e wants a man to take an' gie un a güde hidin'—zame as he oughter give 'is fly-be-night of a wife. [STRANGWAY in his dark clothes has entered, and stands by the door, his lips compressed to a colourless line, his thin, darkish face grey-white] Zame as a man wid ha' gi'en the doctor, for takin' what isn't his'n.

All but JARLAND have seen STRANGWAY. He steps forward, JARLAND sees him now; his jaw drops a little, and he is silent.

STRANGWAY. I came for a little brandy, Mr. GODLEIGH—feeling rather faint. Afraid I mightn't get through the service.

GODLEIGH. [With professional composure] Marteil's Three Star, zurr, or 'Ennessy's?

STRANGWAY. [Looking at JARLAND] Thank you; I believe I can do without, now. [He turns to go.

In the deadly silence, GODLEIGH touches the arm of JARLAND, who, leaning against the bar with the pewter in his hand, is staring with his strange lowering eyes straight at STRANGWAY.

JARLAND. [Galvanized by the touch into drunken rage] Lave me be—I'll talk to un—parson or no. I'll tache un to meddle wi' my maid's bird. I'll tache un to kape 'is thievin' 'ands to 'imself.

[STRANGWAY turns again.

CLYST. Be quiet, Tam.

JARLAND. [Never loosing STRANGWAY with his eyes—like a bull-dog who sees red] That's for one chake; zee un turn t'other, the white-livered büty! Whü lets another man 'ave 'is wife, an' never the sperit to go vor un!

BURLACOMBE. Shame, Jarland; quiet, man!

They are all looking at STRANGWAY, who, under JARLAND's drunken insults is standing rigid, with his eyes closed, and his hands hard clenched. The church bell has stopped slow ringing, and begun its five minutes' hurrying note.

TRUSTAFORD. [Rising, and trying to hook his arm into JARLAND's] Come away, Tam; yü've a-'ad tü much, man.

JARLAND. [Shaking him off] Zee, 'e darsen't touch me; I might 'it un in the vace an' 'e darsen't; 'e's afraid—like 'e was o' the doctor.

He raises the pewter as though to fling it, but it is seized by GODLEIGH from behind, and falls clattering to the floor. STRANGWAY has not moved.

JARLAND. [Shaking his fist almost in his face] Lüke at un, lüke at un! A man wi' a slut for a wife—

As he utters the word "wife" STRANGWAY seizes the outstretched fist, and with a ju-jitsu movement, draws him into his clutch, helpless. And as they sway and struggle in the open window, with the false strength of fury he forces JARLAND through. There is a crash of broken glass from outside. At the sound STRANGWAY comes to himself. A look of agony passes over his face. His eyes light on Jim Bere, who has suddenly risen, and stands feebly clapping his hands. STRANGWAY rushes out.

Excitedly gathering at the window, they all speak at once.

CLYST. Tarn's hatchin' of yüre cucumbers, Mr. GODLEIGH.

TRUSTAFORD. 'E did crash; haw, haw!

FREMAN. 'Twas a brave throw, zürely. Whü wid a' thought it?

CLYST. Tam's crawlin' out. [Leaning through window] Hallo, Tam—'ow's t' base, old man?

FREMAN. [Excitedly] They'm all comin' up from churchyard to zee.

TRUSTAFORD. Tam dü lüke wonderful aztonished; haw, haw! Poor old Tam!

CLYST. Can yü zee curate? Rackon 'e'm gone into church. Aw, yes; gettin' a bit dimsy—sarvice time. [A moment's hush.

TRUSTAFORD. Well, I'm jiggered. In 'alf an hour he'm got to prache.

GODLEIGH. 'Tes a Christian village, boys.

Feebly, quietly, JIM BERE laughs. There is silence; but the bell is heard still ringing.

SCENE II

The same—in daylight dying fast. A lamp is burning on the bar. A chair has been placed in the centre of the room, facing the bench under the window, on which are seated from right to left, GODLEIGH, SOL POTTER the village shopman, TRUSTAFORD, BURLACOMBE, FREMAN, JIM BERE, and MORSE the blacksmith. CLYST is squatting on a stool by the bar, and at the other end JAR-LAND, sobered and lowering, leans against the lintel of the porch leading to the door, round which are gathered five or six sturdy fellows, dumb as fishes. No one sits in the chair. In the unnatural silence that reigns, the distant sound of the wheezy church organ and voices singing can be heard.

TRUSTAFORD. [After a prolonged clearing of his throat] What I mean to zay is that 'tes no yüse, not a bit o' yüse in the world, not düin' of things properly. If an' in case we'm to carry a resolution disapprovin' o' curate, it must all be done so as no one can't zay nothin'.

SOL POTTER. That's what I zay, Mr. Trustaford; ef so be as 'tis to be a village meetin', then it must be all done proper.

FREMAN. That's right, Sol Potter. I purpose Mr. Sol Potter into the chair. Whü seconds that?

A silence. Voices from among the dumb-as-fishes: "I dü."

CLYST. [Excitedly] Yü can't putt that to the meetin'. Only a chairman can putt it to the meetin'. I purpose that Mr. Burlacombe—bein' as how he's chairman o' the Parish Council—take the chair.

FREMAN. Ef so be as I can't putt it, yü can't putt that neither.

TRUSTAFORD. 'Tes not a bit o' yüse; us can't 'ave no meetin' without a chairman.

GODLEIGH. Us can't 'ave no chairman without a meetin' to elect un, that's züre. [A silence.

MORSE. [Heavily] To my way o' thinkin', Mr. GODLEIGH speaks zense; us must 'ave a meetin' before us can 'ave a chairman.

CLYST. Then what we got to dü's to elect a meetin'.

BURLACOMBE. [Sourly] Yü'll not find no procedure for that.

Voices from among the dumb-as-fishes: "Mr. Burlacombe 'e oughter know."

SOL POTTER. [Scratching his head—with heavy solemnity] 'Tes my belief there's no other way to dü, but to elect a chairman to call a meetin'; an' then for that meetin' to elect a chairman.

CLYST. I purpose Mr. Burlacombe as chairman to call a meetin'.

FREMAN. I purpose Sol Potter.

GODLEIGH. Can't 'ave tü propositions together before a meetin'; that's apple-pie züre vur zurtain.

Voice from among the dumb-as-fishes: "There ain't no meetin' yet, Sol Potter zays."

TRUSTAFORD. Us must get the rights of it zettled some'ow. 'Tes like the darned old chicken an' the egg—meetin' or chairman—which come virst?

SOL POTTER. [Conciliating] To my thinkin' there shid be another way o' düin' it, to get round it like with a circumbendibus. 'T'all comes from takin' different vüse, in a manner o' spakin'.

FREMAN. Yü goo an' zet in that chair.

SOL POTTER. [With a glance at BURLACOMBE— modestly] I shid'n never like fur to dü that, with Mr. Burlacombe zettin' there.

BURLACOMBE. [Rising] 'Tes all darned fülishness.

Amidst an uneasy shufflement of feet he moves to the door, and goes out into the darkness.

CLYST. [Seeing his candidate thus depart] Rackon curate's pretty well thrü by now, I'm goin' to zee. [As he passes JARLAND] 'Ow's ta base, old man?

[He goes out.

One of the dumb-as-fishes moves from the door and fills the space left on the bench by BURLACOMBE'S departure.

JARLAND. Darn all this puzzivantin'! [To SOL POTTER] Goo an' zet in that chair.

SOL POTTER. [Rising and going to the chair; there he stands, changing from one to the other of his short broad feet and sweating from modesty and worth] 'Tes my düty now, gentlemen, to call a meetin' of the parishioners of this parish. I beg therefore to declare that this is a meetin' in accordance with my duty as chairman of this meetin' which elected me chairman to call this meetin'. And I purceed to vacate the chair so that this meetin' may now purceed to elect a chairman.

He gets up from the chair, and wiping the sweat from his brow, goes back to his seat.

FREMAN. Mr. Chairman, I rise on a point of order.

GODLEIGH. There ain't no chairman.

FREMAN. I don't give a darn for that. I rise on a point of order.

GODLEIGH. 'Tes a chairman that decides points of order. 'Tes certain yü can't rise on no points whatever till there's a chairman.

TRUSTAFORD. 'Tes no yüse yüre risin', not the least bit in the world, till there's some one to zet yü down again. Haw. haw!

Voice from the dumb-as-fishes: "Mr. Trustaford 'e's right."

FREMAN. What I zay is the chairman ought never to 'ave vacated the chair till I'd risen on my point of order. I purpose that he goo and zet down again.

GODLEIGH. Yü can't purpose that to this meetin'; yü can only purpose that to the old meetin' that's not zettin' any longer.

FREMAN. [Excitedly] I don' care what old meetin' 'tis that's zettin'. I purpose that Sol Potter goo an' zet in that chair again, while I rise on my point of order.

TRUSTAFORD. [Scratching his head] 'Tesn't regular—but I guess yü've got to goo, Sol, or us shan't 'ave no peace.

SOL POTTER, still wiping his brow, goes back to the chair.

MORSE. [Stolidly—to FREMAN] Zet down, Will FREMAN. [He pulls at him with a blacksmith's arm.

FREMAN. [Remaining erect with an effort] I'm not a-goin' to zet down till I've arisen.

JARLAND. Now then, there 'e is in the chair. What's yüre point of order?

FREMAN. [Darting his eyes here and there, and flinging his hand up to his gipsy-like head] 'Twas—'twas—Darned ef y' 'aven't putt it clean out o' my 'ead.

JARLAND. We can't wait for yüre points of order. Come out o' that chair, Sol Potter.

SOL POTTER rises and is about to vacate the chair.

FREMAN. I know! There ought to 'a been minutes taken. Yü can't 'ave no meetin' without minutes. When us comes to electin' a chairman o' the next meetin', 'e won't 'ave no minutes to read.

SOL POTTER. 'Twas only to putt down that I was elected chairman to elect a meetin' to elect a chairman to preside over a meetin' to pass a resolution dalin' wi' the curate. That's aisy set down, that is.

FREMAN. [Mollified] We'll 'ave that zet down, then, while we're electin' the chairman o' the next meetin'.

[A silence.

TRUSTAFORD. Well then, seein' this is the praaper old meetin' for carryin' the resolution about the curate, I purpose Mr. Sol Potter take the chair.

FREMAN. I purpose Mr. Trustaford. I 'aven't a-got nothin' against Sol Potter, but seein' that he elected the meetin' that's to elect 'im, it might be said that 'e was electin' of himzelf in a manner of spakin'. Us don't want that said.

MORSE. [Amid meditative grunts from the dumb-as-fishes] There's some-at in that. One o' they tü purposals must be putt to the meetin'.

FREMAN. Second must be putt virst, fur züre.

TRUSTAFORD. I dunno as I wants to zet in that chair. To hiss the curate, 'tis a ticklish sort of a job after that. Vurst comes afore second, Will Freman.

FREMAN. Second is amendment to virst. 'Tes the amendments is putt virst.

TRUSTAFORD. 'Ow's that, Mr. Godleigh? I'm not particular eggzac'ly to a dilly zort of a point like that.

SOL POTTER. [Scratching his head] 'Tes a very nice point, for züre.

GODLEIGH. 'Tes undoubtedly for the chairman to decide.

Voice from the dumb-as-fishes: "But there ain't no chairman yet."

JARLAND. Sol Potter's chairman.

FREMAN. No, 'e ain't.

MORSE. Yes, 'e is—'e's chairman till this second old meetin' gets on the go.

FREMAN. I deny that. What dü yü say, Mr. Trustaford?

TRUSTAFORD. I can't 'ardly tell. It dü zeem a darned long-sufferin' sort of a business altogether.

[A silence.

MORSE. [Slowly] Tell 'ee what 'tis, us shan't dü no güde like this.

GODLEIGH. 'Tes for Mr. Freman or Mr. Trustaford, one or t'other to withdraw their motions.

TRUSTAFORD. [After a pause, with cautious generosity] I've no objections to withdrawin' mine, if Will Freman'll withdraw his'n.

FREMAN. I won't never be be'indhand. If Mr. Trustaford withdraws, I withdraws mine.

MORSE. [With relief] That's zensible. Putt the motion to the meetin'.

SOL POTTER. There ain't no motion left to putt.

[Silence of consternation. [In the confusion JIM BERE is seen to stand up.

GODLEIGH. Jim Bere to spake. Silence for Jim!

VOICES. Aye! Silence for Jim!

SOL POTTER. Well, Jim?

JIM. [Smiling and slow] Nothin' düin'.

TRUSTAFORD. Bravo, Jim! Yü'm right. Best zense yet!

[Applause from the dumb-as-fishes. [With his smile brightening, JIM resumes his seat.

SOL POTTER. [Wiping his brow] Dü seem to me, gentlemen, seein' as we'm got into a bit of a tangle in a manner of spakin', 'twid be the most zimplest and vairest way to begin all over vrom the beginnin', so's t'ave it all vair an' square for every one.

In the uproar of "Aye" and "No," it is noticed that TIBBY JARLAND is standing in front of her father with her finger, for want of something better, in her mouth.

TIBBY. [In her stolid voice] Please, sister Mercy says, curate 'ave got to "Lastly." [JARLAND picks her up, and there is silence.] An' please to come quick.

JARLAND. Come on, mates; quietly now!

[He goes out, and all begin to follow him.

MORSE. [Slowest, save for SOL POTTER] 'Tes rare lucky us was all agreed to hiss the curate afore us began the botherin' old meetin', or us widn' 'ardly 'ave 'ad time to settle what to dü.

SOL POTTER, [Scratching his head] Aye, 'tes rare lucky, but I dunno if 'tes altogether reg'lar.

SCENE II

The village green before the churchyard and the yew-trees at the gate. Into the pitch dark under the yews, light comes out through the half-open church door. Figures are lurking, or moving stealthily—people waiting and listening to the sound of a voice speaking in the church words that are inaudible. Excited whispering and faint giggles come from the deepest yew-tree shade, made ghostly by the white faces and the frocks of young girls continually flitting up and back in the blackness. A girl's figure comes flying out from the porch, down the path of light, and joins the stealthy group.

WHISPERING VOICE OF MERCY. Where's 'e got to now, Gladys?

WHISPERING VOICE OF GLADYS. 'E've just finished.

VOICE OF CONNIE. Whü pushed t'door open?

VOICE OF GLADYS. Tim Clyst—I giv' it a little push, meself.
VOICE OF CONNIE. Oh!
VOICE OF GLADYS. Tim Clyst's gone in!
ANOTHER VOICE. O-o-o-h!
VOICE OF MERCY. Whü else is there, tü?
VOICE OF GLADYS. Ivy's there, an' old Mrs. Potter, an' tü o' the maids from th'Hall; that's all as ever.
VOICE OF CONNIE. Not the old grey mare?
VOICE OF GLADYS. No. She ain't ther'. 'Twill just be th'ymn now, an' the Blessin'. Tibby gone for 'em?
VOICE OF MERCY. Yes.
VOICE OF CONNIE. Mr. Burlacombe's gone in home, I saw 'im pass by just now—'e don' like it. Father don't like it neither.
VOICE OF MERCY. Mr. Strangway shouln' 'ave taken my skylark, an' thrown father out o' winder. 'Tis goin' to be awful fun! Oh!

> She jumps up and down in the darkness. And a voice from far in the shadow says: "Hsssh! Quiet, yü maids!" The voice has ceased speaking in the church. There is a moment's dead silence. The voice speaks again; then from the wheezy little organ come the first faint chords of a hymn.

GLADYS. "Nearer, my God, to Thee!"
VOICE OF MERCY. 'Twill be funny, with no one 'ardly singin'.

> The sound of the old hymn sung by just six voices comes out to them rather sweet and clear.

GLADYS. [Softly] 'Tis pretty, tü. Why! They're only singin' one verse!

> A moment's silence, and the voice speaks, uplifted, pronouncing the Blessing: "The peace of God—" As the last words die away, dark figures from the inn approach over the grass, till quite a crowd seems standing there without a word spoken. Then from out the church porch come the congregation. TIM CLYST first, hastily lost among the waiting figures in the dark; old Mrs. Potter, a half-blind old lady groping her way and perceiving nothing out of the ordinary; the two maids from the Hall, self-conscious and scared, scuttling along. Last, IVY BURLACOMBE quickly, and starting back at the dim, half-hidden crowd.

VOICE OF GLADYS. [Whispering] Ivy! Here, quick! IVY sways, darts off towards the voice, and is lost in the shadow.

VOICE OF FREMAN. [Low] Wait, boys, till I give signal.

Two or three squirks and giggles; TIM CLYST'S voice: "Ya-as! Don't 'ee tread on my toe!" A soft, frightened "O-o-h!" from a girl. Some quick, excited whisperings:

"Luke!" "Zee there!" "He's comin'!" And then a perfectly dead silence. The figure of STRANGWAY is seen in his dark clothes, passing from the vestry to the church porch. He stands plainly visible in the lighted porch, locking the door, then steps forward. Just as he reaches the edge of the porch, a low hiss breaks the silence. It swells very gradually into a long, hissing groan. STRANGWAY stands motionless, his hand over his eyes, staring into the darkness. A girl's figure can be seen to break out of the darkness and rush away. When at last the groaning has died into sheer expectancy, STRANGWAY drops his hand.

STRANGWAY. [In a low voice] Yes! I'm glad. Is Jarland there?

FREMAN. He's 'ere—no thanks to yü! Hsss!

[The hiss breaks out again, then dies away.

JARLAND'S VOICE. [Threatening] Try if yü can dü it again.

STRANGWAY. No, Jarland, no! I ask you to forgive me. Humbly!

[A hesitating silence, broken by muttering.

CLYST'S VOICE. Bravo!

A VOICE. That's vair!

A VOICE 'E's afraid o' the sack—that's what 'tis.

A VOICE. [Groaning] 'E's a praaper coward.

A VOICE. Whü funked the doctor?

CLYST'S VOICE. Shame on 'ee, therr!

STRANGWAY. You're right—all of you! I'm not fit! An uneasy and excited muttering and whispering dies away into renewed silence.

STRANGWAY. What I did to Tarn Jarland is not the real cause of what you're doing, is it? I understand. But don't be troubled. It's all over. I'm going—you'll get some one better. Forgive me, JARLAND. I can't see your face—it's very dark.

FREMAN'S VOICE. [Mocking] Wait for the full müne.

GODLEIGH. [Very low] "My 'eart 'E lighted not!"

STRANGWAY. [Starting at the sound of his own words thus mysteriously given him out of the darkness] Whoever found that, please tear it up! [After a moments silence] Many of you have been very kind to me. You won't see me again—Good-bye, all!

He stands for a second motionless, then moves resolutely down into the darkness so peopled with shadows.

UNCERTAIN VOICES AS HE PASSES. Good-bye, zurr! Good luck, zurr! [He has gone.

CLYST'S VOICE. Three cheers for Mr. Strangway! And a queer, strangled cheer, with groans still threading it, arises.

ACT III

SCENE I

In the BURLACOMBES' hall-sittingroom the curtains are drawn, a lamp burns, and the door stands open. BURLACOMBE and his wife are hovering there, listening to the sound of mingled cheers and groaning.

MRS. BURLACOMBE. Aw! my güdeness—what a thing t'appen! I'd süner 'a lost all me ducks. [She makes towards the inner door] I can't never face 'im.

BURLACOMBE. 'E can't expect nothin' else, if 'e act like that.

MRS. BURLACOMBE. 'Tes only düin as 'e'd be done by.

BURLACOMBE. Aw! Yü can't go on forgivin' 'ere, an' forgivin' there. 'Tesn't nat'ral.

MRS. BURLACOMBE. 'Tes the mischief 'e'm a parson. 'Tes 'im bein' a lamb o' God—or 'twidden be so quare for 'im to be forgivin'.

BURLACOMBE. Yü goo an' make un a güde 'ot drink.

MRS. BURLACOMBE. Poor soul! What'll 'e dü now, I wonder? [Under her breath] 'E's comin'!

She goes hurriedly. BURLACOMBE, with a startled look back, wavers and makes to follow her, but stops undecided in the inner doorway. STRANG-

WAY comes in from the darkness. He turns to the window and drops overcoat and hat and the church key on the window-seat, looking about him as men do when too hard driven, and never fixing his eyes long enough on anything to see it. BURLACOMBE. closing the door into the house, advances a step. At the sound STRANGWAY faces round.

BURLACOMBE. I wanted for yü to know, zurr, that me an' mine 'adn't nothin' to dü wi' that darned fülishness, just now.

STRANGWAY. [With a ghost of a smile] Thank you, Burlacombe. It doesn't matter. It doesn't matter a bit.

BURLACOMBE. I 'ope yü won't take no notice of it. Like a lot o' silly bees they get. [After an uneasy pause] Yü'll excuse me spakin' of this mornin', an' what 'appened. 'Tes a brave pity it cam' on yü so sudden-like before yü 'ad time to think. 'Tes a sort o' thing a man shüde zet an' chew upon. Certainly 'tes not a bit o' yüse goin' against human nature. Ef yü don't stand up for yüreself there's no one else not goin' to. 'Tes yüre not 'avin' done that 'as made 'em so rampageous. [Stealing another look at STRANGWAY] Yü'll excuse me, zurr, spakin' of it, but 'tes amazin' sad to zee a man let go his own, without a word o' darin'. 'Tes as ef 'e'ad no passions-like.

STRANGWAY. Look at me, Burlacombe.

BURLACOMBE looks up, trying hard to keep his eyes on STRANGWAY'S, that seem to burn in his thin face.

STRANGWAY. Do I look like that? Please, please! [He touches his breast] I've too much here. Please!

BURLACOMBE. [With a sort of startled respect] Well, zurr, 'tes not for me to zay nothin', certainly.

He turns and after a slow look back at STRANGWAY goes out.

STRANGWAY. [To himself] Passions! No passions! Ha!

The outer door is opened and Ivy BURLACOMBE appears, and, seeing him, stops. Then, coming softly towards him, she speaks timidly.

Ivy. Oh! Mr. Strangway, Mrs. Bradmere's comin' from the Rectory. I ran an' told 'em. Oh! 'twas awful.

STRANGWAY starts, stares at her, and turning on his heel, goes into the house. IVY's face is all puckered, as if she were on the point of tears. There is a gentle scratching at the door, which has not been quite closed.

VOICE OF GLADYS. [Whispering] Ivy! Come on! Ivy. I won't.

VOICE OF MERCY. Yu must. Us can't dü without yü.

Ivy. [Going to the door] I don't want to.

VOICE OF GLADYS. "Naughty maid, she won't come out," Ah! dü 'ee!

VOICE OF CONNIE. Tim Clyst an' Bobbie's comin'; us'll only be six anyway. Us can't dance "figure of eight" without yü.

Ivy. [Stamping her foot] I don't want to dance at all! I don't.

MERCY. Aw! She's temper. Yü can bang on tambourine, then!

GLADYS. [Running in] Quick, Ivy! Here's the old grey mare comin' down the green. Quick.

With whispering and scuffling, gurgling and squeaking, the reluctant Ivy's hand is caught and she is jerked away. In their haste they have left the door open behind them.

VOICE OF MRS. BRADMERE. [Outside] Who's that? She knocks loudly, and rings a bell; then, without waiting, comes in through the open door.

Noting the overcoat and hat on the window-sill she moves across to ring the bell. But as she does so, MRS. BURLACOMBE, followed by BURLACOMBE, comes in from the house.

MRS. BRADMERE. This disgraceful business! Where's MR. STRANGWAY? I see he's in.

MRS. BURLACOMBE. Yes, m'm, he'm in—but—but Burlacombe dü zay he'm terrible upzet.

MRS. BRADMERE. I should think so. I must see him—at once.

MRS. BURLACOMBE. I doubt bed's the best place for 'un, an' a güde 'ot drink. Burlacombe zays he'm like a man standin' on the edge of a cliff, and the laste tipsy o' wind might throw un over.

MRS. BRADMERE. [To BURLACOMBE] You've seen him, then?

BURLACOMBE. Yeas; an' I don't like the lüke of un—not a little bit, I don't.

MRS. BURLACOMBE. [Almost to herself] Poor soul; 'e've a-'ad tü much to try un this yer long time past. I've a-seen 'tis sperrit comin' thrü 'is body, as yü might zay. He's torn to bits, that's what 'tis.

BURLACOMBE. 'Twas a praaper cowardly thing to hiss a man when he's down. But 'twas natural tü, in a manner of spakin'. But 'tesn't that troublin' 'im. 'Tes in here [touching his forehead], along of his wife, to my thinkin'. They zay 'e've a-known about 'er afore she went away. Think of what 'e've 'ad to kape in all this time. 'Tes enough to drive a man silly after that. I've a-locked my gun up. I see a man lüke like that once before—an' sure enough 'e was dead in the mornin'!

MRS. BRADMERE. Nonsense, Burlacombe! [To MRS. BURLACOMBE] Go and tell him I want to see him—must see him. [MRS. BURLACOMBE goes into the house] And look here, Burlacombe; if we catch any one, man or woman, talking of this outside the village, it'll be the end of their tenancy, whoever they may be. Let them all know that. I'm glad he threw that drunken fellow out of the window, though it was a little—

BURLACOMBE. Aye! The nüspapers would be praaper glad of that, for a tiddy bit o' nüse.

MRS. BRADMERE. My goodness! Yes! The men are all up at the inn. Go and tell them what I said— it's not to get about. Go at once, Burlacombe.

BURLACOMBE. Must be a turrable job for 'im, every one's knowin' about 'is wife like this. He'm a proud man tü, I think. 'Tes a funny business altogether!

MRS. BRADMERE. Horrible! Poor fellow! Now, come! Do your best, Burlacombe!

BURLACOMBE touches his forelock and goes. MRS. BRADMERE stands quite still, thinking. Then going to the photograph, she stares up at it.

MRS. BRADMERE. You baggage!

STRANGWAY has come in noiselessly, and is standing just behind her. She turns, and sees him. There is something so still, so startlingly still in his figure and white face, that she cannot for the moment find her voice.

MRS. BRADMERE. [At last] This is most distressing. I'm deeply sorry. [Then, as he does not answer, she goes a step closer] I'm an old woman; and old women must take liberties, you know, or they couldn't get on at all. Come now! Let's try and talk it over calmly and see if we can't put things right.

STRANGWAY. You were very good to come; but I would rather not.

MRS. BRADMERE. I know you're in as grievous trouble as a man can be.
STRANGWAY. Yes.
MRS. BRADMERE. [With a little sound of sympathy] What are you—thirty-five? I'm sixty-eight if I'm a day—old enough to be your mother. I can feel what you must have been through all these months, I can indeed. But you know you've gone the wrong way to work. We aren't angels down here below! And a son of the Church can't act as if for himself alone. The eyes of every one are on him.
STRANGWAY. [Taking the church key from the window-sill] Take this, please.
MRS. BRADMERE. No, no, no! Jarland deserved all he got. You had great provocation—
STRANGWAY. It's not Jarland. [Holding out the key] Please take it to the Rector. I beg his forgiveness. [Touching his breast] There's too much I can't speak of—can't make plain. Take it to him, please.
MRS. BRADMERE. Mr. Strangway—I don't accept this. I am sure my husband—the Church—will never accept—
STRANGWAY. Take it!
MRS. BRADMERE. [Almost unconsciously taking it] Mind! We don't accept it. You must come and talk to the Rector to-morrow. You're overwrought. You'll see it all in another light, then.
STRANGWAY. [With a strange smile] Perhaps. [Lifting the blind] Beautiful night! Couldn't be more beautiful!
MRS. BRADMERE. [Startled—softly] Don't turn away from those who want to help you! I'm a grumpy old woman, but I can feel for you. Don't try and keep it all back, like this! A woman would cry, and it would all seem clearer at once. Now won't you let me—?
STRANGWAY. No one can help, thank you.
MRS. BRADMERE. Come! Things haven't gone beyond mending, really, if you'll face them. [Pointing to the photograph] You know what I mean. We dare not foster immorality.
STRANGWAY. [Quivering as at a jabbed nerve] Don't speak of that!
MRS. BRADMERE. But think what you've done, Mr. Strangway! If you can't take your wife back, surely you must divorce her. You can never help her to go on

like this in secret sin.

STRANGWAY. Torture her—one way or the other?

MRS. BRADMERE. No, no; I want you to do as the Church—as all Christian society would wish. Come! You can't let this go on. My dear man, do your duty at all costs!

STRANGWAY. Break her heart?

MRS. BRADMERE. Then you love that woman—more than God!

STRANGWAY. [His face quivering] Love!

MRS. BRADMERE. They told me—Yes, and I can see you're in a bad way. Come, pull yourself together ! You can't defend what you're doing.

STRANGWAY. I do not try.

MRS. BRADMERE. I must get you to see! My father was a clergyman; I'm married to one; I've two sons in the Church. I know what I'm talking about. It's a priest's business to guide the people's lives.

STRANGWAY. [Very low] But not mine! No more!

MRS. BRADMERE. [Looking at him shrewdly] There's something very queer about you to-night. You ought to a see doctor.

STRANGWAY. [A smile coming and going on his lips] If I am not better soon—

MRS. BRADMERE. I know it must be terrible to feel that everybody—[A convulsive shiver passes over STRANGWAY, and he shrinks against the door] But come! Live it down! [With anger growing at his silence] Live it down, man! You can't desert your post—and let these villagers do what they like with us? Do you realize that you're letting a woman, who has treated you abominably—yes, abominably—go scot-free, to live comfortably with another man? What an example!

STRANGWAY. Will you, please, not speak of that!

MRS. BRADMERE. I must! This great Church of ours is based on the rightful condemnation of wrongdoing. There are times when forgiveness is a sin, Michael Strangway. You must keep the whip hand. You must fight!

STRANGWAY. Fight! [Touching his heart] My fight is here. Have you ever been in hell? For months and months—burned and longed; hoped against hope; killed a man in thought day by day? Never rested, for love and hate? I—condemn! I—judge! No! It's rest I have to find—somewhere—somehow—rest! And how—

how can I find rest?

MRS. BRADMERE. [Who has listened to his outburst in a sort of coma] You are a strange man! One of these days you'll go off your head if you don't take care.

STRANGWAY. [Smiling] One of these days the flowers will grow out of me; and I shall sleep.

MRS. BRADMERE stares at his smiling face a long moment in silence, then with a little sound, half sniff, half snort, she goes to the door. There she halts.

MRS. BRADMERE. And you mean to let all this go on—Your wife—

STRANGWAY. Go ! Please go!

MRS. BRADMERE. Men like you have been buried at cross-roads before now! Take care! God punishes!

STRANGWAY. Is there a God ?

MRS. BRADMERE. Ah! [With finality] You must see a doctor.

Seeing that the look on his face does not change, she opens the door, and hurries away into the moonlight.

STRANGWAY crosses the room to where his wife's picture hangs, and stands before it, his hands grasping the frame. Then he takes it from the wall, and lays it face upwards on the window-seat.

STRANGWAY. [To himself] Gone! What is there, now?

The sound of an owl's hooting is floating in, and of voices from the green outside the inn.

STRANGWAY. [To himself] Gone! Taken faith—hope—life!

JIM BERE comes wandering into the open doorway.

JIM BERE. Güde avenin', zurr.

At his slow gait, with his feeble smile, he comes in, and standing by the window-seat beside the long dark coat that still lies. there, he looks down at STRANGWAY with his lost eyes.

JIM. Yü threw un out of winder. I cud 'ave, once, I cud. [STRANGWAY neither moves nor speaks; and JIM BERE goes on with his unimaginably slow speech] They'm laughin' at yü, zurr. An' so I come to tell 'ee how to dü. 'Twas full müne—when I caught 'em, him an' my girl. I caught 'em. [With a strange and awful flash of fire] I did; an' I tuk un [He takes up STRANGWAY'S coat and grips it with his trembling hands, as a man grips another's neck] like that—I tuk un.

As the coat falls, like a body out of which the breath has been squeezed, STRANGWAY, rising, catches it.

STRANGWAY. [Gripping the coat] And he fell!

He lets the coat fall on the floor, and puts his foot on it. Then, staggering back, he leans against the window.

JIM. Yü see, I loved 'er—I did. [The lost look comes back to his eyes] Then somethin'—I dunno—and—and—[He lifts his hand and passes it up and down his side] 'Twas like this for ever.

[They gaze at each other in silence.

JIM. [At last] I come to tell yü. They'm all laughin' at yü. But yü'm strong—yü go over to Durford to that doctor man, an' take un like I did. [He tries again to make the sign of squeezing a man's neck] They can't laugh at yü no more, then. Tha's what I come to tell yü. Tha's the way for a Christian man to dü. Güde naight, zurr. I come to tell yee.

STRANGWAY motions to him in silence. And, very slowly, JIM BERE passes out.

The voices of men coming down the green are heard.

VOICES. Güde naight, Tam. Güde naight, old Jim!

VOICES. Güde naight, Mr. Trustaford. 'Tes a wonderful fine müne.

VOICE OF TRUSTAFORD. Ah! 'Tes a brave müne for th' poor old curate!

VOICE. "My 'eart 'E lighted not!"

TRUSTAFORD's laugh, and the raffling, fainter and fainter, of wheels. A spasm seizes on STRANGWAY'S face, as he stands there by the open door, his hand grips his throat; he looks from side to side, as if seeking a way of escape.

SCENE II

THE BURLACOMBES' high and nearly empty barn. A lantern is hung by a rope that lifts the bates of straw, to a long ladder leaning against a rafter. This gives all the light there is, save for a slender track of moonlight, slanting in from the end, where the two great doors are not quite closed. On a rude bench in front of a few remaining, stacked, square-cut bundles of last year's hay, sits TIBBY JARLAND, a bit of apple in her mouth, sleepily beating on a tambourine. With stockinged feet GLADYS, IVY, CONNIE, and MERCY, TIM CLYST, and BOBBIE JARLAND, a boy of fifteen, are dancing a truncated "Figure of Eight"; and their shadows are dancing alongside on the walls. Shoes and some apples have been thrown down close to the side door through which they have come in. Now and then Ivy, the smallest and best of the dancers, ejaculates words of direction, and one of the youths grunts or breathes loudly out of the confusion of his mind. Save for this and the dumb beat and jingle of the sleepy tambourine, there is no sound. The dance comes to its end, but the drowsy TIBBY goes on beating.

MERCY. That'll dü, Tibby; we're finished. Ate yüre apple. [The stolid TIBBY eats her apple.

CLYST. [In his teasing, excitable voice] Yü maids don't dance 'alf's well as us dü. Bobbie 'e's a great dancer. 'E dance vine. I'm a güde dancer, meself.

GLADYS. A'n't yü conceited just?

CLYST. Aw! Ah! Yü'll give me kiss for that. [He chases, but cannot catch that slippery white figure] Can't she glimmer!

MERCY. Gladys! Up ladder!

CLYST. Yü go up ladder; I'll catch 'ee then. Naw, yü maids, don't yü give her succour. That's not vair.

[Catching hold of Mercy, who gives a little squeal.

CONNIE. Mercy, don't! Mrs. Burlacombe'll hear. Ivy, go an' peek.

[IVY goes to the side door and peers through.

CLYST. [Abandoning the chase and picking up an apple—they all have the joyous irresponsibility that attends forbidden doings] Ya-as, this is a güde apple. Lüke at Tibby!

TIBBY, overcome by drowsiness, has fallen back into the hay, asleep. GLADYS, leaning against the hay breaks into humming:

"There cam' three dükes a-ridin', a-ridin', a-ridin', There cam' three dükes a ridin' With a ransy-tansy tay!"

CLYST. Us 'as got on vine; us'll get prize for our dancin'.

CONNIE. There won't be no prize if Mr. Strangway goes away. 'Tes funny 'twas Mrs. Strangway started us.

IVY. [From the door] 'Twas wicked to hiss him.
[A moment's hush.
CLYST. 'Twasn't I.
BOBBIE. I never did.
GLADYS. Oh! Bobbie, yü did! Yü blew in my ear.
CLYST. 'Twas the praaper old wind in the trees. Did make a brave noise, zurely.
MERCY. 'E shuld'n' 'a let my skylark go.
CLYST. [Out of sheer contradictoriness] Ya-as, 'e shüde, then. What dü yü want with th' birds of the air? They'm no güde to yü.
IVY. [Mournfully] And now he's goin' away.
CLYST. Ya-as; 'tes a pity. He's the best man I ever seen since I was comin' from my mother. He's a güde man. He'm got a zad face, sure enough, though.
IVY. Güde folk always 'ave zad faces.
CLYST. I knü a güde man—'e sold pigs—very güde man: 'e 'ad a büdiful bright vace like the müne. [Touching his stomach] I was sad, meself, once. 'Twas a funny scrabblin'-like feelin'.
GLADYS. If 'e go away, whü's goin' to finish us for confirmation?
CONNIE. The Rector and the old grey mare.
MERCY. I don' want no more finishin'; I'm confirmed enough.
CLYST. Ya-as; yü'm a büty.
GLADYS. Suppose we all went an' asked 'im not to go?
IVY. 'Twouldn't be no güde.
CONNIE. Where's 'e goin'?
MERCY. He'll go to London, of course.
IVY. He's so gentle; I think 'e'll go to an island, where there's nothin' but birds and beasts and flowers.
CLYST. Aye! He'm awful fond o' the dumb things.
IVY. They're kind and peaceful; that's why.
CLYST. Aw! Yü see ttt praaper old torn cats; they'm not tü peaceful, after that, nor kind naighther.
BOBBIE. [Surprisingly] If 'e's sad, per'aps 'e'll go to 'Eaven.
IVY. Oh! not yet, Bobbie. He's tü young.

CLYST. [Following his own thoughts] Ya-as. 'Tea a funny place, tü, nowadays, judgin' from the papers.

GLADYS. Wonder if there's dancin' in 'Eaven?

IVY. There's beasts, and flowers, and waters, and trees—'e told us.

CLYST. Naw! There's no dumb things in 'Eaven. Jim Bere 'e says there is! 'E thinks 'is old cat's there.

IVY. Yes. [Dreamily] There's stars, an' owls, an' a man playin' on the flute. Where 'tes güde, there must be müsic.

CLYST. Old brass band, shuldn' wonder, like th' Salvation Army.

IVY. [Putting up her hands to an imaginary pipe] No; 'tis a boy that goes so; an' all the dumb things an' all the people goo after 'im—like this.

 She marches slowly, playing her imaginary pipe, and one by one they all fall in behind her, padding round the barn in their stockinged feet. Passing the big doors, IVY throws them open.

An' 'tes all like that in 'Eaven.

 She stands there gazing out, still playing on her imaginary pipe. And they all stand a moment silent, staring into the moonlight.

CLYST. 'Tes a glory-be full müne to-night!

IVY. A goldie-cup—a big one. An' millions o' little goldie-cups on the floor of 'Eaven.

MERCY. Oh! Bother 'Eaven! Let's dance "Clapperclaws" ! Wake up, Tibby!

GLADYS. Clapperclaws, clapperclaws! Come on, Bobbie—make circle!

CLYST. Clapperclaws! I dance that one fine.

IVY. [Taking the tambourine] See, Tibby; like this. She hums and beats gently, then restores the tambourine to the sleepy TIBBY, who, waking, has placed a piece of apple in her mouth.

CONNIE. 'Tes awful difficult, this one.

IVY. [Illustrating] No; yü just jump, an' clap yüre 'ands. Lovely, lovely!

CLYST. Like ringin' bells! Come ahn!

TIBBY begins her drowsy beating, IVY hums the tune; they dance, and their shadows dance again upon the walls. When she has beaten but a few moments on the tambourine, TIBBY is overcome once more by sleep and falls back again into her nest of hay, with her little shoed feet just visible over the edge of the bench. IVY catches up the tambourine, and to her beating and humming the dancers dance on.

Suddenly GLADYS stops like a wild animal surprised, and cranes her neck towards the side door.

CONNIE. [Whispering] What is it?

GLADYS. [Whispering] I hear—some one—comin' across the yard.

She leads a noiseless scamper towards the shoes. BOBBIE JARLAND shins up the ladder and seizes the lantern. IVY drops the tambourine. They all fly to the big doors, and vanish into the moonlight, pulling the doors nearly to again after them.

There is the sound of scrabbling at the latch of the side door, and STRANGWAY comes into the nearly dark barn. Out in the night the owl is still hooting. He closes the door, and that sound is lost. Like a man walking in his sleep, he goes up to the ladder, takes the rope in his hand, and makes a noose. He can be heard breathing, and in the darkness the motions of his hands are dimly seen, freeing his throat and putting the noose round his neck. He stands swaying to and fro at the foot of the ladder; then, with a sigh, sets his foot on it to mount. One of the big doors creaks and opens in the wind, letting in a broad path of moonlight.

STRANGWAY stops; freeing his neck from the noose, he walks quickly up the track of moonlight, whitened from head to foot, to close the doors.

The sound of his boots on the bare floor has awakened TIBBY JARLAND. Struggling out of her hay nest she stands staring at his whitened figure, and bursts suddenly into a wail.

TIBBY. O-oh! Mercy! Where are yü? I'm frightened! I'm frightened! O-oooo!

STRANGWAY. [Turning—startled] Who's that? Who is it?

TIBBY. O-oh! A ghosty! Oo-ooo!

STRANGWAY. [Going to her quickly] It's me, Tibby—Tib—only me!

Tibby. I see'd a ghosty.

STRANGWAY. [Taking her up] No, no, my bird, you didn't! It was me.

TIBBY. [Burying her face against him] I'm frighted. It was a big one. [She gives tongue again] O-o-oh!

STRANGWAY. There, there! It's nothing but me. Look!

TIBBY. No. [She peeps out all the same.

STRANGWAY. See! It's the moonlight made me all white. See! You're a brave girl now ?

TIBBY. [Cautiously] I want my apple.

   She points towards her nest. STRANGWAY carries her there, picks up an apple, and gives it her. TIBBY takes a bite.

TIBBY. I want my tambouline.

STRANGWAY. [Giving her the tambourine, and carrying her back into the track of moonlight] Now we're both ghosties! Isn't it funny ?

TIBBY. [Doubtfully] Yes.

STRANGWAY. See! The moon's laughing at us! See? Laugh then!

TIBBY, tambourine in one hand and apple in the other, smiles stolidly. He sets her down on the ladder, and stands, holding her level with him.

TIBBY. [Solemnly] I'se still frightened.

STRANGWAY. No! Full moon. Tibby! Shall we wish for it ?

TIBBY. Full müne.

STRANGWAY. Moon! We're wishing for you. Moon, moon!

TIBBY. Müne, we're wishin' for yü!

STRANGWAY. What do you wish it to be?

TIBBY. Bright new shillin'!

STRANGWAY. A face.

TIBBY. Shillin', a shillin'!

STRANGWAY. [Taking out a shilling and spinning it so that it falls into her pinafore] See! Your wish comes true.

TIBBY. Oh! [Putting the shilling in her mouth] Müne's still there!

STRANGWAY. Wish for me, Tibby!

TIBBY. Müne, I'm wishin' for yü!

STRANGWAY. Not yet!

TIBBY. Shall I shake my tambouline ?

STRANGWAY. Yes, shake your tambouline.

TIBBY. [Shaking her tambourine] Müne, I'm shakin' at yü.

STRANGWAY lays his hand suddenly on the rope, and swings it up on to the beam.

TIBBY. What d'yü dü that for?

STRANGWAY. To put it out of reach. It's better—

TIBBY. Why is it better? [She stares up at him.

STRANGWAY. Come along, Tibby! [He carries her to

www.bookjungle.com *email: sales@bookjungle.com fax: 630-214-0564 mail: Book Jungle PO Box 2226 Champaign, IL 61825*

The Codes Of Hammurabi And Moses
W. W. Davies

QTY

The discovery of the Hammurabi Code is one of the greatest achievements of archaeology, and is of paramount interest, not only to the student of the Bible, but also to all those interested in ancient history...

Religion **ISBN:** *1-59462-338-4* *Pages:132*
MSRP $12.95

The Theory of Moral Sentiments
Adam Smith

QTY

This work from 1749. contains original theories of conscience amd moral judgment and it is the foundation for systemof morals.

Philosophy **ISBN:** *1-59462-777-0* *Pages:536*
MSRP $19.95

Jessica's First Prayer
Hesba Stretton

QTY

In a screened and secluded corner of one of the many railway-bridges which span the streets of London there could be seen a few years ago, from five o'clock every morning until half past eight, a tidily set-out coffee-stall, consisting of a trestle and board, upon which stood two large tin cans, with a small fire of charcoal burning under each so as to keep the coffee boiling during the early hours of the morning when the work-people were thronging into the city on their way to their daily toil...

Childrens **ISBN:** *1-59462-373-2* *Pages:84*
MSRP $9.95

My Life and Work
Henry Ford

QTY

Henry Ford revolutionized the world with his implementation of mass production for the Model T automobile. Gain valuable business insight into his life and work with his own auto-biography... "We have only started on our development of our country we have not as yet, with all our talk of wonderful progress, done more than scratch the surface. The progress has been wonderful enough but..."

Biographies/ **ISBN:** *1-59462-198-5* *Pages:300*
MSRP $21.95

www.bookjungle.com *email: sales@bookjungle.com fax: 630-214-0564 mail: Book Jungle PO Box 2226 Champaign, IL 61825*

The Art of Cross-Examination
Francis Wellman

QTY

I presume it is the experience of every author, after his first book is published upon an important subject, to be almost overwhelmed with a wealth of ideas and illustrations which could readily have been included in his book, and which to his own mind, at least, seem to make a second edition inevitable. Such certainly was the case with me; and when the first edition had reached its sixth impression in five months, I rejoiced to learn that it seemed to my publishers that the book had met with a sufficiently favorable reception to justify a second and considerably enlarged edition. ...

Reference   ISBN: *1-59462-647-2*   Pages:412   MSRP *$19.95*

On the Duty of Civil Disobedience
Henry David Thoreau

QTY

Thoreau wrote his famous essay, On the Duty of Civil Disobedience, as a protest against an unjust but popular war and the immoral but popular institution of slave-owning. He did more than write—he declined to pay his taxes, and was hauled off to gaol in consequence. Who can say how much this refusal of his hastened the end of the war and of slavery ?

Law   ISBN: *1-59462-747-9*   Pages:48   MSRP *$7.45*

Dream Psychology Psychoanalysis for Beginners
Sigmund Freud

QTY

Sigmund Freud, born Sigismund Schlomo Freud (May 6, 1856 - September 23, 1939), was a Jewish-Austrian neurologist and psychiatrist who co-founded the psychoanalytic school of psychology. Freud is best known for his theories of the unconscious mind, especially involving the mechanism of repression; his redefinition of sexual desire as mobile and directed towards a wide variety of objects; and his therapeutic techniques, especially his understanding of transference in the therapeutic relationship and the presumed value of dreams as sources of insight into unconscious desires.

Psychology   ISBN: *1-59462-905-6*   Pages:196   MSRP *$15.45*

The Miracle of Right Thought
Orison Swett Marden

QTY

Believe with all of your heart that you will do what you were made to do. When the mind has once formed the habit of holding cheerful, happy, prosperous pictures, it will not be easy to form the opposite habit. It does not matter how improbable or how far away this realization may see, or how dark the prospects may be, if we visualize them as best we can, as vividly as possible, hold tenaciously to them and vigorously struggle to attain them, they will gradually become actualized, realized in the life. But a desire, a longing without endeavor, a yearning abandoned or held indifferently will vanish without realization.

Self Help   ISBN: *1-59462-644-8*   Pages:360   MSRP *$25.45*

www.bookjungle.com email: sales@bookjungle.com fax: 630-214-0564 mail: Book Jungle PO Box 2226 Champaign, IL 61825

QTY

	Title	ISBN	Price
☐	**The Rosicrucian Cosmo-Conception Mystic Christianity** by *Max Heindel*	ISBN: *1-59462-188-8*	**$38.95**
	The Rosicrucian Cosmo-conception is not dogmatic, neither does it appeal to any other authority than the reason of the student. It is: not controversial, but is: sent forth in the, hope that it may help to clear...		New Age/Religion Pages 646
☐	**Abandonment To Divine Providence** by *Jean-Pierre de Caussade*	ISBN: *1-59462-228-0*	**$25.95**
	"The Rev. Jean Pierre de Caussade was one of the most remarkable spiritual writers of the Society of Jesus in France in the 18th Century. His death took place at Toulouse in 1751. His works have gone through many editions and have been republished..."		Inspirational/Religion Pages 400
☐	**Mental Chemistry** by *Charles Haanel*	ISBN: *1-59462-192-6*	**$23.95**
	Mental Chemistry allows the change of material conditions by combining and appropriately utilizing the power of the mind. Much like applied chemistry creates something new and unique out of careful combinations of chemicals the mastery of mental chemistry...		New Age Pages 354
☐	**The Letters of Robert Browning and Elizabeth Barret Barrett 1845-1846 vol II** by *Robert Browning and Elizabeth Barrett*	ISBN: *1-59462-193-4*	**$35.95**
			Biographies Pages 596
☐	**Gleanings In Genesis (volume I)** by *Arthur W. Pink*	ISBN: *1-59462-130-6*	**$27.45**
	Appropriately has Genesis been termed "the seed plot of the Bible" for in it we have, in germ form, almost all of the great doctrines which are afterwards fully developed in the books of Scripture which follow...		Religion/Inspirational Pages 420
☐	**The Master Key** by *L. W. de Laurence*	ISBN: *1-59462-001-6*	**$30.95**
	In no branch of human knowledge has there been a more lively increase of the spirit of research during the past few years than in the study of Psychology, Concentration and Mental Discipline. The requests for authentic lessons in Thought Control, Mental Discipline and...		New Age/Business Pages 422
☐	**The Lesser Key Of Solomon Goetia** by *L. W. de Laurence*	ISBN: *1-59462-092-X*	**$9.95**
	This translation of the first book of the "Lernegton" which is now for the first time made accessible to students of Talismanic Magic was done, after careful collation and edition, from numerous Ancient Manuscripts in Hebrew, Latin, and French...		New Age/Occult Pages 92
☐	**Rubaiyat Of Omar Khayyam** by *Edward Fitzgerald*	ISBN:*1-59462-332-5*	**$13.95**
	Edward Fitzgerald, whom the world has already learned, in spite of his own efforts to remain within the shadow of anonymity, to look upon as one of the rarest poets of the century, was born at Bredfield, in Suffolk, on the 31st of March, 1809. He was the third son of John Purcell...		Music Pages 172
☐	**Ancient Law** by *Henry Maine*	ISBN: *1-59462-128-4*	**$29.95**
	The chief object of the following pages is to indicate some of the earliest ideas of mankind, as they are reflected in Ancient Law, and to point out the relation of those ideas to modern thought.		Religion/History Pages 452
☐	**Far-Away Stories** by *William J. Locke*	ISBN: *1-59462-129-2*	**$19.45**
	"Good wine needs no bush, but a collection of mixed vintages does. And this book is just such a collection. Some of the stories I do not want to remain buried for ever in the museum files of dead magazine-numbers an author's not unpardonable vanity..."		Fiction Pages 272
☐	**Life of David Crockett** by *David Crockett*	ISBN: *1-59462-250-7*	**$27.45**
	"Colonel David Crockett was one of the most remarkable men of the times in which he lived. Born in humble life, but gifted with a strong will, an indomitable courage, and unremitting perseverance...		Biographies/New Age Pages 424
☐	**Lip-Reading** by *Edward Nitchie*	ISBN: *1-59462-206-X*	**$25.95**
	Edward B. Nitchie, founder of the New York School for the Hard of Hearing, now the Nitchie School of Lip-Reading, Inc, wrote "LIP-READING Principles and Practice". The development and perfecting of this meritorious work on lip-reading was an undertaking...		How-to Pages 400
☐	**A Handbook of Suggestive Therapeutics, Applied Hypnotism, Psychic Science** by *Henry Munro*	ISBN: *1-59462-214-0*	**$24.95**
			Health/New Age/Health/Self-help Pages 376
☐	**A Doll's House: and Two Other Plays** by *Henrik Ibsen*	ISBN: *1-59462-112-8*	**$19.95**
	Henrik Ibsen created this classic when in revolutionary 1848 Rome. Introducing some striking concepts in playwriting for the realist genre, this play has been studied the world over.		Fiction/Classics/Plays 308
☐	**The Light of Asia** by *sir Edwin Arnold*	ISBN: *1-59462-204-3*	**$13.95**
	In this poetic masterpiece, Edwin Arnold describes the life and teachings of Buddha. The man who was to become known as Buddha to the world was born as Prince Gautama of India but he rejected the worldly riches and abandoned the reigns of power when...		Religion/History/Biographies Pages 170
☐	**The Complete Works of Guy de Maupassant** by *Guy de Maupassant*	ISBN: *1-59462-157-8*	**$16.95**
	"For days and days, nights and nights, I had dreamed of that first kiss which was to consecrate our engagement, and I knew not on what spot I should put my lips..."		Fiction/Classics Pages 240
☐	**The Art of Cross-Examination** by *Francis L. Wellman*	ISBN: *1-59462-309-0*	**$26.95**
	Written by a renowned trial lawyer, Wellman imparts his experience and uses case studies to explain how to use psychology to extract desired information through questioning.		How-to/Science/Reference Pages 408
☐	**Answered or Unanswered?** by *Louisa Vaughan*	ISBN: *1-59462-248-5*	**$10.95**
	Miracles of Faith in China		Religion Pages 112
☐	**The Edinburgh Lectures on Mental Science (1909)** by *Thomas*	ISBN: *1-59462-008-3*	**$11.95**
	This book contains the substance of a course of lectures recently given by the writer in the Queen Street Hall, Edinburgh. Its purpose is to indicate the Natural Principles governing the relation between Mental Action and Material Conditions...		New Age/Psychology Pages 148
☐	**Ayesha** by *H. Rider Haggard*	ISBN: *1-59462-301-5*	**$24.95**
	Verily and indeed it is the unexpected that happens! Probably if there was one person upon the earth from whom the Editor of this, and of a certain previous history, did not expect to hear again...		Classics Pages 380
☐	**Ayala's Angel** by *Anthony Trollope*	ISBN: *1-59462-352-X*	**$29.95**
	The two girls were both pretty, but Lucy who was twenty-one who supposed to be simple and comparatively unattractive, whereas Ayala was credited, as her Bombwhat romantic name might show, with poetic charm and a taste for romance. Ayala when her father died was nineteen...		Fiction Pages 484
☐	**The American Commonwealth** by *James Bryce*	ISBN: *1-59462-286-8*	**$34.45**
	An interpretation of American democratic political theory. It examines political mechanics and society from the perspective of Scotsman James Bryce		Politics Pages 572
☐	**Stories of the Pilgrims** by *Margaret P. Pumphrey*	ISBN: *1-59462-116-0*	**$17.95**
	This book explores pilgrims religious oppression in England as well as their escape to Holland and eventual crossing to America on the Mayflower, and their early days in New England...		History Pages 268

www.bookjungle.com *email:* sales@bookjungle.com *fax:* 630-214-0564 *mail:* Book Jungle PO Box 2226 Champaign, IL 61825

QTY

The Fasting Cure by **Sinclair Upton** ISBN: *1-59462-222-1* **$13.95**
In the Cosmopolitan Magazine for May, 1910, and in the Contemporary Review (London) for April, 1910, I published an article dealing with my experiences in fasting. I have written a great many magazine articles, but never one which attracted so much attention... New Age/Self Help/Health Pages 164

Hebrew Astrology by **Sepharial** ISBN: *1-59462-308-2* **$13.45**
In these days of advanced thinking it is a matter of common observation that we have left many of the old landmarks behind and that we are now pressing forward to greater heights and to a wider horizon than that which represented the mind-content of our progenitors... Astrology Pages 144

Thought Vibration or The Law of Attraction in the Thought World ISBN: *1-59462-127-6* **$12.95**
by **William Walker Atkinson** Psychology/Religion Pages 144

Optimism by **Helen Keller** ISBN: *1-59462-108-X* **$15.95**
Helen Keller was blind, deaf, and mute since 19 months old, yet famously learned how to overcome these handicaps, communicate with the world, and spread her lectures promoting optimism. An inspiring read for everyone... Biographies/Inspirational Pages 84

Sara Crewe by **Frances Burnett** ISBN: *1-59462-360-0* **$9.45**
In the first place, Miss Minchin lived in London. Her home was a large, dull, tall one, in a large, dull square, where all the houses were alike, and all the sparrows were alike, and where all the door-knockers made the same heavy sound... Childrens/Classic Pages 88

The Autobiography of Benjamin Franklin by **Benjamin Franklin** ISBN: *1-59462-135-7* **$24.95**
The Autobiography of Benjamin Franklin has probably been more extensively read than any other American historical work, and no other book of its kind has had such ups and downs of fortune. Franklin lived for many years in England, where he was agent... Biographies/History Pages 332

Name	
Email	
Telephone	
Address	
City, State ZIP	

☐ Credit Card   ☐ Check / Money Order

Credit Card Number	
Expiration Date	
Signature	

Please Mail to: Book Jungle
PO Box 2226
Champaign, IL 61825
or Fax to: 630-214-0564

ORDERING INFORMATION

web: *www.bookjungle.com*
email: *sales@bookjungle.com*
fax: 630-214-0564
mail: *Book Jungle PO Box 2226 Champaign, IL 61825*
or PayPal *to sales@bookjungle.com*

Please contact us for bulk discounts

DIRECT-ORDER TERMS

**20% Discount if You Order
Two or More Books**
Free Domestic Shipping!
Accepted: Master Card, Visa,
Discover, American Express

www.ingramcontent.com/pod-product-compliance
Lightning Source LLC
Chambersburg PA
CBHW081329040426
42453CB00013B/2348